USS Saratoga

Written by David Doyle

Squadron At Sea

Squadron Signal
Publications

Cover Art by Don Greer

Line Illustrations by Todd Sturgell

(Front Cover) USS *Saratoga* was the third aircraft carrier operated by the U.S. Navy. Serving through the duration of WWII, the *Saratoga* wore at number of different camouflage schemes during the conflict, including this disruptive pattern in late 1944.

(Back Cover) Fabric-covered biplanes were the standard when *Saratoga* was commissioned, and her career would end with an atomic blast. Young men of *Saratoga's* early crews would become the leaders of U.S. carrier forces during WWII.

About the Squadron At Sea Series®

The *Squadron At Sea* series details a specific ship using color and black-and-white archival photographs and photographs of in-service, preserved, and restored equipment. *Squadron At Sea* titles are devoted to civilian and military vessels, while *On Deck*® titles are devoted to warships. These picture books focus on specific vessels from the laying of the keel to present or its finale.

Proudly printed in the U.S.A.
Copyright 2013 Squadron/Signal Publications
1115 Crowley Drive, Carrollton, TX 75006-1312 U.S.A.

Hard Cover ISBN 978-0-89747-711-6
Soft Cover ISBN 978-0-89747-712-3

Military/Combat Photographs and Snapshots

If you have any photos of aircraft, armor, soldiers, or ships of any nation, particularly wartime snapshots, please share them with us and help make Squadron/Signal's books all the more interesting and complete in the future. Any photograph sent to us will be copied and returned. Electronic images are preferred. The donor will be fully credited for any photos used. Please send them to:

Squadron/Signal Publications
1115 Crowley Drive
Carrollton, TX 75006-1312 U.S.A.
www.SquadronSignalPublications.com

USS *Saratoga* (CV-3), originally laid down in 1920 as a battlecruiser, was completed in 1927 as an aircraft carrier. She served throughout WWII, three times being severely damaged in combat, and following the war sank following her use – twice – as a target for atomic bomb tests. (National Museum of Naval Aviation)

Dedication

To the crew of the *Saratoga* – the Ship of Happy Landings – who helped pioneer naval aviation in peacetime, fought valiantly in wartime, and who brought many of their comrades safely home; and to the memory of their fallen shipmates, who gave all defending their nation, their ship, and their buddies.

Introduction

When the keel of the *Saratoga* was laid down on 25 September 1920, she, along with her sister ships, were intended to be the most powerful battlecruisers in the world. Authorized by the Naval Act of 1916, the new class of battlecruisers – *Lexington, Constellation, Saratoga, Ranger, Constitution,* and *United States,* along with the six *South Dakota* (BB-49)-class battleships begun at the same time, would catapult the U.S. Navy into being one of the, if not the singular, most powerful fleet in the world.

Originally designed to be armed with ten 14-inch, 50-caliber rifles, by the time construction of the ships had got under way the intended armament had been changed to eight 16-inch, 50-caliber rifles. In terms of naval weaponry, the caliber of the gun is the barrel length divided by the bore – thus a 16-inch, 50-caliber gun barrel is 800 inches long. Battlecruiser design theory was to create a very heavily armed, relatively lightly armored, warship which relied upon unusually high speed as a key element of its defense. The *Lexingtons* were designed to steam at 35-knots, a pace unheard of at the time for such a large vessel. To attain this pace would require a whopping 180,000 horsepower, six times more powerful than the largest machinery the U.S. Navy had built up to that time, the 29,000 horsepower *West Virginia* (BB-48). The *Lexingtons* were to displace 43,500 tons each, making them the heaviest ships in the fleet.

The signing of the Washington Naval Treaty on 6 February 1922, however, spelled the end of the U.S. battlecruiser plans. The treaty required the immediate suspension of capital ship construction, although it did permit each signatory to use two existing capital ship hulls as the basis for aircraft carriers, with a displacement not to exceed 33,000 tons each (vs. the 27,000-ton limit otherwise imposed on carriers). *Lexington,* CC-1, under construction at Fore River Shipyard, Quincy, Massachusetts; and *Saratoga,* CC-3, being built by New York Shipbuilding, Camden, New Jersey, were 24.2 percent and 28 percent complete, repectively, when construction was suspended in February 1922. As the two battlecruisers nearest completion, they were selected for conversion to aircraft carriers. The rest of the class, which ranged in completion from 22.7 percent for the *Constellation* to 4 percent for *Ranger,* were scrapped on the builders' ways.

Independently of all of this, the Navy had been experimenting on an assortment of new aircraft carrier designs, including one with a projected displacement of 39,000 tons and a length of 850 feet, whose preliminary design was delivered 5 May 1921. When the treaty was signed, it took only until 17 February 1922 to adapt the 1921 design to the *Lexington*-class hull. However, largely to meet the Treaty-imposed weight limitations, this design required further refinement, and it was 21 December 1923 before final plans were approved and the yards were told to proceed with the conversion of the two vessels, retaining their names but changing their hull numbers to CV-2 and CV-3.

Despite the additional 6,000 ton Treaty allowance given these ships as compared to new-construction aircraft carriers, there was considerable concern regarding hitting the weight requirement. In fact, a clause in the treaty permitted the modernization of existing capital ships for additional protection against underwater and air attacks; with an allowance of 3000 tons per ship for this protection. The Navy argued that the *Lexingtons*

The keel of the *Saratoga*, U.S. Navy battlecruiser, is laid at the New York Shipbuilding Corporation's shipyard at Camden, New Jersey, on 25 September 1920. Workers are guiding the keel onto wooden blocks. (Naval History and Heritage Command)

Acknowledgments

Warships, particularly capital ships, touch many lives, their complexity, long service life and considerable range bring them into contact with many more people than does, for example, a single tank or specific airplane. Accordingly, archival resources concerning the *Saratoga* were scattered from coast to coast and through the collections of many individuals and institutions, many which generously opened their resources for the creation of this book.

I would like to thank fellow authors Tom Kailbourn, Robert C. Stern, John Fry, A.D. Baker III, and Scott Taylor for their help with this project. Researchers Tracy White, Martin Quinn, Jerry Leslie, Roger Torgeson, Rick Davis, Patty Anderson, and James Noblin were very generous in sharing their discoveries with me. The archival resources of the National Archives, at College Park, Maryland; San Bruno, California; and Seattle, Washington yielded many treasures of information, as did the Hawaii State Archives, National Museum of Naval Aviation, San Diego Air and Space Museum, Puget Sound Naval Shipyard, various branches of the National Park Service, including the National Park Service Submerged Resources Unit, Hampton Roads Naval Museum, U.S. Naval Institute, The Floating Drydock, and Maritme Quest. Robert Hanshew and Chuck Haberlein at the Naval History and Heritage Command were generous with their time and providing access to the collection to complete this study.

The dedicated staff at Squadron Signal Publications have invested long hours in reviving worn and faded photographs, and ensuring that my words not only are accurate, but would not horrify my former English teachers. My darling wife Denise scanned hundreds of images and sifted through thousands of pages of dusty documents helping to pull together the materials presented here.

All photos not otherwise credited are from the collection of the U.S. National Archives and Records Administration, College Park, Maryland.

fell into this category, and thus their actual tonnage was 36,000.

After some delays in construction, primarily due to continued haggling over the weight limit, *Saratoga* was finally launched on 7 April 1925. Tugs nudged her immense hull into New York Ship's huge fitting out wet barn extending into the Delaware River near her builder's ways. There, an army of laborers swarmed over her for the next two years, until finally on 16 November 1927 she was commissioned, officially becoming "USS" *Saratoga*. Once commissioned, she was moved across the river to Philadelphia Navy Yard for a final fitting out, then on 6 January 1928 cast off and began her shakedown cruise. Two days out, on 8 January, *Saratoga's* aircraft made their first flight. With *Saratoga's* navigator Charles Pownall at the controls, a Vought UO-1 equipped with floats was lowered into the water, and soon took off – in the back seat, *Saratoga's* first Air Officer, Lieutenant Commander Marc Mitscher.

Three days later, on 11 January, it was Mitscher at the controls of a UO-1, this time without floats, when the first flight was made from *Saratoga's* deck. After Mitscher returned to the ship, three additional flights were made that day by Charles Mason, John Price, and Frederick Pennoyer, all Lieutenant Commanders. Less than two weeks later, while anchored off the U.S. Naval War College, Newport, Rhode Island, bad weather began overtaking the vessel, by 0255 on 24 January *Saratoga* was steaming ahead ⅓ just to maintain her position, even though all three anchors had been lowered. This was Sara's first encounter with the fury of the sea, but it would not be her last.

On 8 March 1922, a panel of U.S. Navy admirals exhibited models of a cruiser (upper) and an aircraft carrier (lower) to members of the House Naval Affairs Committee to explain how cruiser hulls under construction could be converted into carriers. (National Museum of Naval Aviation)

An artist's conception depicts a *Lexington*-class ship as completed as a battle cruiser. Of the six ships originally planned for this class, only two, *Lexington* and *Saratoga*, were completed, but during their construction they were converted to aircraft carriers.

A month after the laying of her keel, the double bottom of the *Saratoga* takes shape in a photo dated 26 October 1920. The construction is viewed from astern. The keel extends to the foreground, and in the background, frame members pierced with lightening holes are in place. Some of the plates of the outer shell, or skin, of the hull have been fastened to the frame members. Only a few workmen are visible here and there.

In another photograph dated 26 October 1920, the progress of construction of the ship is viewed from the bow, looking aft. Fore-and-aft frame members called longitudinals are in place. Later, the stem, or the vertical frame at the bow, would begin to take shape in the foreground. Rising to each side of the building ways are scaffolds, which the workmen would use as the sides of the hull were constructed progressively upward.

The bow of the *Saratoga* is in the initial stages of construction in the foreground. Numerous transverse and longitudinal bulkheads have been installed since the photographs on the preceding page was taken. On the sides of the hull, adjacent to the scaffolding, the side frames are in the process of being erected; these were raised in sections. Three rows of tanks for fuel and water are visible on each side of the hull.

The *Saratoga* under construction is viewed from astern in April 1921. In the amidships area are the machinery spaces, where the turbines and generators that will power the ship will be installed. To the sides of the longitudinal bulkheads, defining the machinery spaces, are the fire rooms, where the boilers will be positioned. In the foreground, the shell plates, which formed the outer skin of the ship, extend above the frame members.

Battlecruiser *Saratoga:* Proposed Specifications

Displacement:	43,500 long tons
Length:	874 feet overall
Beam:	105 feet 4 inches
Draft:	31 feet
Installed power:	180,000 shp
Propulsion:	four shafts, turbo-electric drive, 16 water-tube boilers
Speed:	33 knots (38 mph)
Range:	10,000 nautical miles at 10 knots
Complement:	1,297 (1,326 as flagship)
Armament:	
	Eight 16-inch/50 caliber guns in four two-gun turrets
	Fourteen 6-inch /53 caliber in single mounts
	Eight 3-inch/50 caliber anti-aircraft guns
	Eight 21-inch torpedo tubes, 4 submerged
Armored belt:	5-7 inches
Barbette armor:	5-9 inches
Deck armor:	1.5-2.25 inches

In the background of this 28 February 1922 photo from the port side of the third deck is the lower part of the barbette for turret number one. Had *Saratoga* been completed as a battle cruiser, barbettes would have been present below the main-battery turrets.

The state of construction on the *Saratoga* is observed from the bow on 1 July 1921. Construction of the stem had not yet begun. In addition to the maze of scaffolding and planks adjacent to the hull, wooden planks and temporary platforms with guard rails are positioned on top of the upper bulkheads and the frame of the ship, upon which workmen are going about their tasks. Many wooden ladders are also visible.

The photographer of the preceding view moved over to the starboard side of the third deck, amidships, to take this view looking toward the bow. Among the markings on the bulkhead to the lower left are "drill 25/32 wire hole" on each side of a center mark.

Another 28 February 1922 photograph, taken from what would become the chief petty officers' quarters on the third deck looking forward, documents the state of construction on the bow, visible in the background. Below are the first platform and bulkhead 33.

As seen from above the bow looking aft on 8 March 1922, construction has advanced to the level of the third deck, with much of the plating for that deck yet to be installed. Resting on the deck is the foundation of the barbette for turret number one. If the *Saratoga* had been completed as a battle cruiser as originally planned, this barbette would have fit into the space to the front of the curve in the plating of the third deck.

Another photograph dated 8 March 1922 taken from an overhead crane shows the foundation of the barbette for turret one at the bottom and the opening for the barbette to the front of it. At the front of that opening, bulkhead 44 has a curve at its center to accommodate the front of the barbette. Barbettes formed armored enclosures for the operating machinery and ammunition-handling areas of the main-battery gun mounts.

This view of the *Saratoga* was taken from an overhead crane above the temporarily positioned foundation of the barbette for turret three, looking forward, probably on 8 March 1922. In the background is the temporarily positioned barbette for turret one. Within the next four months, these barbettes would be rendered moot when plans were approved to convert the *Saratoga* from a battle cruiser to an aircraft carrier.

This final photograph from the series of overhead views taken on 8 March 1922 faces aft from amidships. In the foreground is the round opening for the barbette of turret three. This opening would be covered when the ship was converted to an aircraft carrier. Lying on the deck beyond the round opening is what appears to be a prefabricated transverse bulkhead awaiting installation.

The *Saratoga* had reached 29.4 percent completion on 1 July 1922 when the U.S. Congress authorized the Navy to convert her and her sister ship, the *Lexington,* to aircraft carriers. In this 30 September 1922 view from above the bow facing aft, work is proceeding on the *Saratoga*. The barbette foundations had been removed from the deck, but the opening for the turret-one barbette is still present in the center of the photo.

A view taken from an overhead crane on 30 September 1922, looking aft, shows in greater detail much of the area that appears in the background of the preceding photograph. The area of the third deck in the immediate foreground would become the well of the forward elevator. Farther aft on each side of the deck are openings in the deck; some of these would accommodate the boiler uptakes, eight on each side of the deck.

Three months after the preceding two photographs were taken, a view from above the aft part of the *Saratoga,* looking forward shows the progress of work on the third deck in the immediate foreground. Beams are exposed where the deck plates have yet to be installed. The beams and the plates were pre-drilled to very exacting tolerances so that rivets could be fastened to them when the plates were positioned on the beams.

The third deck from amidships toward the bow is in the foreground in this 2 April 1923 photograph of the *Saratoga* taken from an overhead crane. Below the exposed beams in the lower part of the photo are the compartments on the first platform (the level below the third deck) for the main driving motors for the two inboard propellers. Just beyond those beams is the round opening originally intended for the barbette for turret one.

Saratoga's third deck is viewed looking forward from amidships on 30 May 1923. In the foreground are several temporary shelters; the overhead crane could lift and move them around when necessary. To each side of the deck are openings for the boiler uptakes. The uptakes were large ductwork assemblies that conducted exhaust fumes from the boilers in the fire rooms up to the four smoke pipes housed within the smokestack.

The forward part of *Saratoga's* third deck is seen facing aft in late June 1923. This deck was of armored construction, to protect the vital machinery and running equipment below. The deck plate that earlier had formed the rear part of the opening for the barbette foundation for turret three has been removed, slightly above the center of the photo, apparently in preparation for covering the opening with a continuous steel plate.

Six months after the preceding photograph was taken, on 2 January 1924, progress is evident in the construction of the amidships area of the *Saratoga*, as viewed from above the bow. In the foreground, several portable shelters and a maze of parts, assemblies, and equipment are arrayed on the third deck. In the background, on a level with the top of the lateral bulkhead, beams have been installed for the second or hangar deck.

On 2 January 1924, a photographer captured this view from the port side of the aft part of the *Saratoga* looking forward. In the foreground and to the right are frame members, atop which further frame members will be attached as construction proceeds.

Another 2 January 1924 photo shows the third deck aft from the port bow. Workmen are engaged in riveting the deck plates to the beams and longitudinal frame members. The plates were temporarily fastened in place with bolts and nuts in advance of riveting.

U.S.S. SARATOGA
BOW LOOKING AFT
N.Y.S. CORP. CAMDEN, N.J.
MARCH 28TH 1924

As seen in this 28 March 1924 photo taken from above the bow facing aft, more bulkheads have been erected on the third deck. Aft of the second lateral bulkhead to the rear of the nearest bulkhead, on each side of the third deck are partitions for chief petty officers' quarters. Rising in the background is the hangar deck. The structure rising to the starboard side of the hangar deck (left in the photo) contains the uptake trunks.

This photo was taken from the scaffolding to the port side of the bow looking starboard and aft on 30 June 1924. In the foreground is a longitudinal bulkhead with temporary wooden braces. To the right, the upper levels of the side of the hull are taking shape.

The interior of the *Saratoga* is observed from above frame 100, looking aft, on 2 October 1924. A key point of reference for finding one's way around a ship forward to aft was by the number of the lateral frame. Frame 100 was close to the midpoint of the ship.

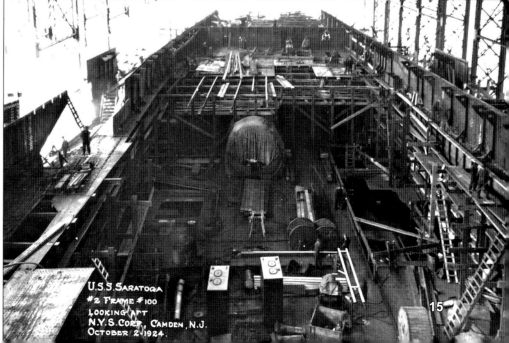

Taken on the same date as the preceding image is this photo from the aft part of the *Saratoga* looking forward. To each side of the hull on the third deck and the hangar deck in the background, the shapes of passageways and storage compartments are visible, and these continued forward past the hangar space. The structure rising to the starboard side of the hangar space (right in the photo) housed the uptakes and vent ducts.

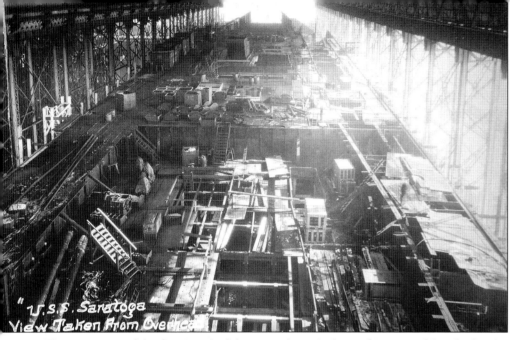

U.S.S. Saratoga
View Taken From Overhead

U.S.S. Saratoga
View Taken From Overhead

The upper part of the *Saratoga* is rising ever closer to the roof trusses of the shed at the New York Shipbuilding Corporation's Camden, New Jersey, yard in early January 1925. This view was taken from above the center of the ship, looking toward the bow.

On 5 January 1925 a photographer took this view of the *Saratoga* from her amidships area, looking aft. To the right is a longitudinal bulkhead with door openings cut through it. To the left is the outward-curving shell of the hull. Stacks of materials are in view.

An early-April 1925 photograph shows the flight deck from frame 75 facing aft. In the foreground is the T-shaped forward elevator well. Construction on the island, or superstructure, has yet to commence to the left of the photograph.

The flight deck, with temporary shelters and the forward elevator well in view, is observed facing forward in a 3 April 1925 photo. To the lower right are openings for two of the updrafts, above which the smokestack will be constructed later.

Flying Deck From Frame 125
Looking Forward. "U.S.S. Saratoga
New York Shipbuilding Corp.
Camden, N.J. April 3rd 1925

This aerial view documented the launching of the *Saratoga* on 7 April 1925. The ship is sliding, stern first, down the ways underneath the southernmost shed in the Middle Yard of the New York Shipbuilding Company's Camden, New Jersey, facility. Newton Creek is at the bottom of the photo; the destroyer yard is on the far side of the creek. The two large building complexes to the lower right were plate-and-angle shops, where steel plates for the ships were bent and drilled (and countersunk if necessary) for rivets.

In a photo taken a moment after the preceding one, a crowd of spectators looks on as the *Saratoga* slides down the double ways and clears the shed. Soon the ship will be completely afloat. The *Saratoga* was the heaviest warship launched up to that time.

Tugboats move into place alongside the *Saratoga* to move her to the shed where she will be fitted-out. The shed and launching ways from which the *Saratoga* has just emerged is at the center of the photograph, with the water tower immediately behind it.

A formation of biplanes flies overhead during the launching of the *Saratoga* on 7 April 1925. The momentum of sliding down the ways is carrying the ship out into the Delaware River. Next, tugboats will be secured to the ship and will guide it into another shed for the fitting-out phase of construction. The hull is riding high in the water because many more structures have yet to be installed inside and on the carrier. During fitting-out, the ship's island, smokestack, and guns will be installed.

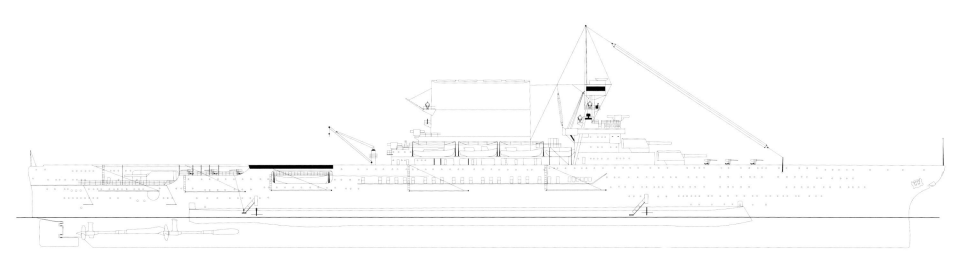

The contract design for the battlecruiser to aircraft carrier conversion, shown here, differed in detail from the final configuration, but was remarkably similar.

A dockside view shows the *Saratoga* being guided by tugboats after her launching. The bow is to the left. A number of people are visible on the flight deck. The four open bays along the upper part of the hull from amidships aft, which will eventually hold the ship's boats, have temporary wooden shoring installed. The shape visible on the flight deck amidships was not a permanent structure but rather a cluster of temporary shelters. (Naval History and Heritage Command)

Tugboats maneuver the *Saratoga* into position to enter a massive "wet barn," or covered wet slip, at the New York Shipbuilding Corporation's Camden, New Jersey, shipyards on 7 April 1925. The light-colored object along the waterline at the bow is the top of the forward poppet, a cradle temporarily secured with cables to the bottom of the bow for the purpose of protecting and guiding the bow during the launching process.

On 21 October 1925, the *Saratoga* is viewed from aft in the wet barn where she is undergoing fitting-out. Exactly one week earlier, the New York Shipbuilding Corporation had been taken over by the Swiss firm of Brown, Boveri & Company, Ltd., and the Camden shipyard subsequently would be renamed the American Brown-Boveri Electrical Corporation. Silhouetted in the opening of the shed, the island is starting to take shape.

The *Saratoga* is viewed from above the aft part of the flight deck, looking forward, on 21 October 1925. In the foreground is the aft elevator well, to the right of which are openings in the flight deck for the uptakes. In the background is the forward elevator well, to the right of which is the island, under construction, with scaffolding erected around it. To the bottom right is the foundation for 8-inch gun mount number three.

Also taken on the same date as the preceding two photographs is this view looking forward of the flight deck of the *Saratoga*. Materials and equipment, including oxygen and acetylene bottles for welding, are grouped on the flight deck. The flight deck was not armored; rather, protection for the ship's vital machinery and control spaces from plunging fire was provided by the third deck, comprising two-inch-thick STS armor.

The original caption of this photo identifies it as a view of the starboard side of the flight deck forward from frame 76 on 1 July 1925. To the lower right are two blurred figures; individuals operating pneumatic drills, boring holes in the steel deck. Within the next several months, the island would be erected in the right foreground. Partly visible beyond the two drillers is an opening in the deck for the barbette of 8-inch gun mount number two.

The fitting-out of the *Saratoga* is proceeding on 31 December 1925 at the by-now renamed American Brown, Boveri Electric Corporation shipyard in Camden, New Jersey. In a view from the stern, the gun houses of the four 8-inch mounts are in place, and the smokestack is in an advanced state of construction, surrounded by scaffolding. The twin 8-inch guns have not yet been installed in turret three but are present in turret four.

The same scene from the preceding photograph is displayed closer-up. To the lower left is the aft port sponson, with mounts present for three 5-inch/25-caliber antiaircraft guns. The guns would be installed on the mounts later. As built, they would carry twelve 5-inch/25-caliber guns in addition to the twin 8-inch/55-caliber guns. The ship would see several successive changes in her defensive armaments in World War II.

Another 31 December 1925 overhead photo shows the forward part of the flight deck, with the forward part of the smokestack under construction to the far right. To the lower right is the aft elevator well. The forward elevator is covered with materials, equipment, and what appear to be temporary windscreens. To the starboard side of the elevator is a temporary boom. On the left side of the hull is staging for the workmen.

Machinery on *Saratoga,* as built

Total Weight:	6,894 tons
Boilers:	Sixteen Babcock & Wilcox; 295 psi, 522 degrees F.
Propulsion turbo-generators:	General Electric, 13-stage, 3 phase, 35,200 kW, 4,980 Volts
Drive motors:	General Electric, squirrel cage, rotor wound, 5,000 volt, two per shaft
Shaft Horsepower:	212,702 during trial; 180,000 design
Maximum Speed:	34.99 knots trial; 33.25 knots design
Lighting / ship's service power plant:	6 General Electric 750kW turbo generators.
Emergency lighting, prior to 1942:	batteries
Endurance:	10 knots : 10,950 miles
Fuel:	2,637 tons oil

The *Saratoga's* smokestack is still surrounded by scaffolding on 1 April 1926. The aft port sponson is seen up close, with the forward gun mount of the three-gun group at the bottom of the photo. Temporary safety rails are installed on the edges of the deck.

The *Saratoga* is viewed from above looking forward on 1 April 1926. A temporary frame to support ladders and scaffolding has been mounted on the ramp at the aft end of the flight deck. A multitude of materials, components, and equipment litter the deck.

It is July 1926 and *Saratoga* has been moved so that her forward half is now outside of the covered wet slip. Dismantling of the scaffold around the smokestack has begun, but much work remains to be done on the island and the structures on the mainmast.

A close examination of this photo dating to around July 1926 indicates that the fir planking on the flight deck has been installed. Temporary ties, rails, and a trolley are present on the port side of the deck for moving heavy equipment and materials.

Tugboats move the unfinished *Saratoga* on 4 September 1926. The shapes of the four boat bays on the port side of the hull are visible. On the front of the smokestack are the secondary conning station and, above it, the aviation control station, or Pri-Fly.

A tugboat operates against the forward starboard part of the *Saratoga*'s hull during the move of the carrier on 4 September 1926. Jutting from the side of the smokestack are two searchlight platforms. The center bow anchor is present but the starboard anchor is not.

Saratoga rests alongside a dock at the American Brown-Boveri Electrical Corporation, Camden, New Jersey, on 4 September 1926. A clear view of the bow is available, including the narrow front end of the flight deck and the temporary guard rails on deck.

The *Saratoga* has been moved so that its forward half is underneath the shed of the covered slip. Above and aft of 8-inch gun turret two, the forms of the navigating bridge and the pilothouse and the fire-control stations on the mainmast are discernible.

The forward part of the *Saratoga* is protected by the shed of a wet slip on 1 April 1927. The three parallel lines on the forward part of the flight deck are the rails of a flywheel aircraft catapult. Two boats are stored to the starboard side of the catapult. Scaffolding is still in place around the structures of the island, mainmast, and smokestack, and masses of construction materials, assemblies, and equipment are still arrayed on the deck.

The starboard side of the *Saratoga* from the smokestack to the stern is displayed in a 1 July 1927 photograph. It appears that the searchlights with light-colored protective covers have been installed on the searchlight platforms on the side of the smokestack.

The *Saratoga* is viewed from the port side on 1 July 1927. The hull has a patchwork appearance, with different colors of paint and primer. Two small platforms over halfway up the smokestack were removed sometime in the next four months.

Saratoga is seen from starboard on 15 November 1927, the day before her commissioning. Below the searchlight platforms on the smokestack is a catwalk from the secondary conning station to the aft main-battery control station at the rear of the stack.

Her forward end ensconced in the shed, *Saratoga*'s port side is displayed in a 15 November 1927 photo. The two small platforms on the funnel seen in the 1 July photo of the *Saratoga*'s port side have been removed, and the whole ship has been painted.

In an undated photograph, *Saratoga* is nearing completion in the wet slip at American Brown, Boveri Electric Corporation shipyard in Camden, New Jersey. The black band around the top of the smokestack would be eliminated by February 1928. (US Naval Institute)

On 27 October 1927, a photographer in an aircraft took this view of the *Saratoga* from her island to her stern. The top of her mainmast and the yardarm extend above the top of the construction shed. It had been 85 months and two days since the keel was laid.

The *Saratoga* is viewed from above the bow in a 15 November 1927 photo. The three rails of the flywheel catapult are prominent in the foreground. Several open hatches are visible on the flight deck in the foreground. Abeam 8-inch turret one, palisades have been erected. These were individual, retractable slats, hinged at the bottom, which were erected to protect the lightweight carrier aircraft of that era from wind damage.

It is now around 9 November 1927, one week before *Saratoga's* commissioning. The carrier displays many details, such as the open vent doors at the stern below the ramp of the flight deck, the flagstaff on the ramp, and boat booms stored against the hull. (US Naval Institute)

Captain Harry E. Yarnell and a host of other officers render honors as the colors are hoisted for the first time aboard *Saratoga* during the 16 November 1927 commissioning ceremony. Construction of the ship had taken more than seven years and cost nearly $44 million, or over $500 million in 2012 dollars. Even then, the ship was not yet ready for operational service; she would spend several months in dry dock at the Philadelphia Navy Yard before her shakedown cruise in early 1928. It had been planned that Captain Henry V. Butler would be *Saratoga's* first captain, but delays in her construction resulted in Captain Yarnell becoming her first skipper.

On 23 November 1927, one week after her commissioning, USS *Saratoga* approaches dry dock at the Philadelphia Navy Yard, across the Delaware River from the American Brown-Boveri Electric Corporation shipyard where the ship was commissioned.

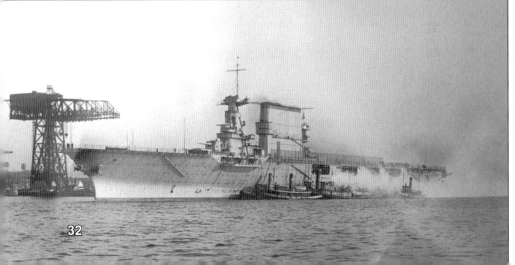

Tugboats assist the newly commissioned USS *Saratoga*. On the starboard side of the front of the flight deck are tracks for a flywheel catapult designed by Carl Norden. The catapult was designed to launch the seaplanes that the *Saratoga* was equipped to deploy in her early years. The paint scheme of the at that time was No. 5 Standard Navy Gray, with No. 20 Standard Deck Gray on steel decks and a mahogany or maroon stain on the flight deck.

The *Saratoga* is viewed a from the starboard side as tugboats ease her across the Delaware River *en route* to drydock at the Philadelphia Navy Yard on 23 November 1927. In dry dock, the lower hull would be scraped and repainted.

The *Saratoga* moves into dry dock at the Philadelphia Navy Yard on 23 November. The narrow front end of the flight deck is apparent. The ship would remain at that yard for the rest of the year, undergoing additional work in preparation for her shakedown cruise.

Part of the port side of USS *Saratoga* is viewed as she is maneuvered into dry dock on 23 November 1927. In the foreground, a team of sailors haul on a mooring hawser. On the sponson on the side of the hull, three 5-inch/25-caliber guns are pointed upward.

In dry dock, a workman standing on a scaffold plank to the lower left works on the port inboard propeller. Aft of the propeller is the rudder, shown turned to the starboard. To the right are draft marks, numbers indicating the distance to the bottom of the keel.

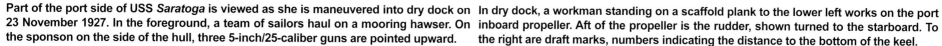

With a large cloud of steam issuing from her smokestack, USS *Saratoga* is moored to a dock at the Philadelphia Navy Yard during her sojourn there in December 1927. The ship was undergoing a final fitting-out before embarking on her shakedown cruise.

The *Saratoga* is observed from a different perspective in a December 1927 photograph. Looming over the carrier is the League Island Crane, a hammerhead crane with a capacity of 350 tons. For many years, this was the U.S. Navy's largest crane.

Situated in dry dock, the *Saratoga* is viewed from her port bow, displaying her bulbous bow and the anchors, including one on the centerline of the bow, encased in the hawse pipes. The anchors were attached to chains that were driven by a windlass on the main deck, immediately below the flight deck. When the anchors were raised, the anchor chains were stored in chain lockers on the upper half deck, below the main deck.

In a final aerial view of *Saratoga* at Philadelphia Navy Yard, the League Island Crane has been swung over the *Saratoga*. The guide lines on the mahogany-colored flight deck were yellow in order to make them highly visible to pilots when landing on the carrier.

During the *Saratoga*'s shakedown cruise, on 8 January 1928, the ship's navigator, Charles Pownall, with Air Officer Marc Mitscher in the back seat, flew the first mission by one of the ship's aircraft, a water takeoff in a Vought UO-1 observation plane.

Three days later, on 11 January 1928, Mitscher piloted the first aircraft to take off from the flight deck of the *Saratoga*, a Vought UO-1 equipped with landing gear. Later that day, three other officers made flights from the *Saratoga* in that plane.

USS *Saratoga* is seen *en route* from Rhode Island to Virginia during her shakedown cruise on 22 January 1928. The view is from the port side. The forward boat bay has been covered, and a black band was present around the top of the smokestack.

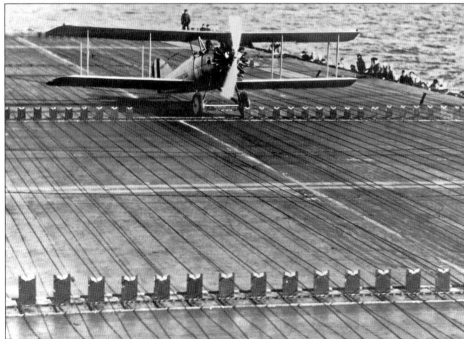

A 6 January 1928 view of the *Saratoga* taken from the forward end of the flight deck includes the two forward twin 8-inch gun mounts, aft of which is the superstructure, or island. Towering above the superstructure and mounted on the tripod foremast are, from bottom to top, the radio-compass booth, the main-battery director, and the control top from which the ship's 5-inch guns were directed. In the foreground are the three tracks of the flywheel catapult for launching seaplanes from the flight deck.

In the late 1920s, a number of advocates for lighter-than-air aircraft advanced the idea that rigid airships used in coastal-patrol activities could be docked and serviced on ships at sea. One such proponent, Navy LCDR Charles Rosendahl, was able to obtain permission to dock the airship USS *Los Angeles* (ZR-3) on the USS *Saratoga*. The attempt was made off the coast of Rhode Island on 27 January 1928. Here, the *Los Angeles* approaches the deck. (Naval History and Heritage Command)

Crewmembers assemble on the fantail of the *Saratoga* as the *Los Angeles* braves 30-knot winds to effect a mooring to the flight deck around 1525 hours on 27 January 1928. Some of the crewmen are handling lines from the *Los Angeles* to ease the airship into place. (Naval History and Heritage Command)

Saratoga made aviation history on 27 January 1928, when she became the first, and only, aircraft carrier to land a dirigible aboard. This historic event was the culmination of an effort by Lt. Cmdr. Charles Rosendahl, a proponent of lighter-than-air craft. Navy officials agreed to the project, so long as this could be done without disrupting *Saratoga's* scheduled repositioning to the West Coast.

The opportunity would present itself on the 27th of the month, although weather conditions were less than ideal, with 30-knot winds. The 656-long airship USS *Los Angeles* (ZR-3), which had been built in Germany, dropped mooring lines to the flight deck of *Saratoga* at 1525 hours, and shortly thereafter drenched the line handlers with ballast water, which had to be jettisoned to counter a gust of wind. Despite the frigid, unexpected, shower, *Saratoga's* crew was able to walk the airship sufficiently forward for *Los Angeles'* control car to land on the carrier's deck, and once secured, *Los Angeles'* executive officer H. V. Wiley stepped from his ship directly aboard *Saratoga*. The press covered this historic event from an escorting destroyer, having agreed only to report the story if the landing was a success.

With the concept proven, *Los Angeles* cast off and returned to her Lakehurst, New Jersey, base. *Saratoga* proceeded to Virginia, embarking Marine Squadron VO-6M and its aircraft, which, in response to the rebellion of Augusto César Sandino, were to be dropped of in Nicaragua, while *Saratoga* steamed on for the U.S. West Coast. Captain Yarnell himself took the con as *Saratoga* was threaded through the locks of the Panama Canal, her 106-foot beam leaving only a two-foot margin, and her antiaircraft gun mounts scraping the lock walls. On 21 February she arrived in Long Beach.

The control car of the *Los Angeles* has alighted on the flight deck of the *Saratoga*. Although the experiment was successful, the concept of landing airships on aircraft carriers was not pursued any further. The *Los Angeles* served with the Navy until 1939. (Naval History and Heritage Command)

During the *Saratoga*'s shakedown cruise in January 1928, the ship was ordered to proceed to the Battle Fleet, currently based at Long Beach, California. This move entailed a transit of the Panama Canal. The *Saratoga* is seen here negotiating the Pedro Miguel Locks of the canal on 7 February 1928, a month and one day after departing Philadelphia Navy Yard. It is apparent from this aerial view that there was very little room to spare between the hull of the *Saratoga* and the sides of the lock; the ship had about two feet of clearance on each side.

Saratoga emerges from the Pedro Miguel Locks in a photo taken moments after the picture on the opposite page. A large, light-colored cover erected over the flight deck amidships gives the crewmen and officers on deck some relief from the tropical sun.

Three days before the two preceding photos were taken, on 4 February 1928, the *Saratoga* passed through the Gatún Locks in the Panama Canal. A good view is provided of the two aft main-battery turrets and, aft of the smokestack, the aft fire-control stations.

A photographer in an aircraft from Naval Air Station Coco Loco took this aerial view of the USS *Saratoga* as it emerged from the San Miguel Locks during the carrier's transit of the Panama Canal on 7 February 1928. The bow is to the left, and the large cover over the flight deck is prominent. Two boats are resting on the flight deck forward of 8-inch turret number one. The rectangular openings of the four smoke pipes in the smokestack are visible.

The *Saratoga* proceeds through the Gatún Locks of the Panama Canal on 4 February 1928. On the stern are three spars which could be deployed to hold a life net. Suspended on the sides of the rear of the flight deck are four 6,000-pound kedge anchors.

Saratoga's stern is seen from the starboard side as the carrier transits the Gatún Locks on 4 February 1928. While negotiating the second and third chambers of the Gatún Locks, some of the ship's 5-inch gun mounts reportedly scraped the sides of the locks.

USS *Saratoga* presents her bow while transiting the Gatún Locks of the Panama Canal. A good view of the narrow front end of the flight deck and of the bow anchors is provided. Resting on the flight deck aft of the boats is a Martin T3M torpedo bomber configured as a floatplane.

The *Saratoga* navigates Gaillard Cut in the Panama Canal in early February 1928. A close examination of the forward 5-inch gun gallery reveals three D-shaped extensions that are folded up; when lowered, they provided the gun crew with extra platform space. (Panama Canal Authority via Maritme Quest)

Her first transit of the Panama Canal completed, *Saratoga* is moored at Balboa on 7 February 1928. Just above the waterline is the top of the armored belt. This belt was 9 feet 4 inches high, tapering in thickness from 7 inches at the top to 5 inches at the bottom.

Anchored off San Pedro, California, USS *Saratoga* celebrated George Washington's birthday, 22 February 1928, by displaying full dress. This practice, conducted on special occasions, entailed flying pennants fore and aft as well as national flags and jacks. (National Museum of Naval Aviation)

The port side of the smokestack of the USS *Saratoga* dominates the left side of this photo overlooking the flight deck facing aft during the February 1928 transit of the Panama Canal. Jutting out from the far end of the smokestack is the aft control platform for the 5-inch guns. On the aft part of the flight deck is a complex installation of arrestor wires, both lateral ones, called pendants, for engaging the aircraft's arrestor hook, and longitudinal wires to engage hooks on the aircraft's landing gear struts to keep the plane from veering to the side when landing. The longitudinal wires were removed from *Saratoga* in May 1929.

The two aft 8-inch/55-caliber Mk. 9 Mod. 1 gun mounts are trained to the port during exercises off the California coast on 22 March 1928. The objects sticking up from the flight deck are hinged "fiddle bridge" supports for the longitudinal arrestor wires.

On the flight deck to the front of the forward elevator are 25 vertical stakes collectively called the palisade. A just-visible pickup truck parked between the aircraft and the smokestack serves as testament to the immense size of *Saratoga.*

F4B-2 bureau number (BuNo) A8638 is assigned to VF-6B "Felix the Cat Squadron" aboard USS *Saratoga.* The F4B-2 had a maximum speed of 186 miles per hour, a range of 570 miles, and its armament consisted of two .30-caliber machine guns and 244 pounds of bombs.

F2B-1 bureau number A7449, side number 2-B-2, was assigned to Bombing Squadron 2B (VF-2B). This squadron, which formerly was VF-2B serving on USS *Langley* (CV-1), was assigned to the *Saratoga* in March 1928 and redesignated VF-2B in July of that year. (San Diego Air and Space Museum)

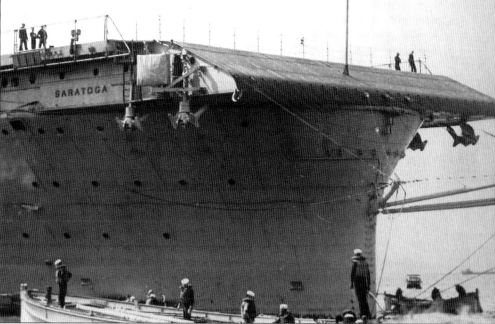

While transiting the Panama Canal on 4 February 1928, sailors of the *Saratoga* are gathered in one of the port-side boat bays, also called boat pockets or compartments. On the ceiling of the bay are two overhead pivoting davits for lowering and raising the craft.

The *Saratoga* presents the port side of her stern during a visit to San Francisco, California on 3 April 1928. The four kedge anchors alongside the rear of the flight deck, each of which weighed three tons, later were removed permanently to save on weight.

A utility motor boat is being lowered from the *Saratoga* in early April 1928. The overhead pivoting-arm davits were swung outward to give the boat, suspended from the boat falls, the necessary clearance to be lowered into the water or raised from the water.

A Martin T3M torpedo bomber mounted on floats rests on the flight deck of the USS *Saratoga* in a view of the ship's forward port beam from early April 1928. A clear view is presented of the forward port 5-inch/25-caliber gun gallery and its three hinged platform extensions.

Lieutenant R. F. Whitehead crashed this Vought UO-1, BuNo A6716, into the barrier on the *Saratoga* on 18 May 1928, surviving the accident. Barrier wires could stop a plane that failed to catch an arrestor wire, but usually not without damage to the plane. (Naval History and Heritage Command)

The *Saratoga* had many appointments that were quite modern for the time, such as this dishwashing machine in the crew's scullery, located on the main deck next to the crew's galley. A rack of dishes is also visible in this photo dated 13 April 1928.

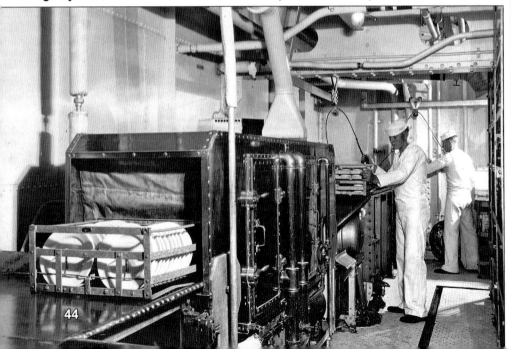

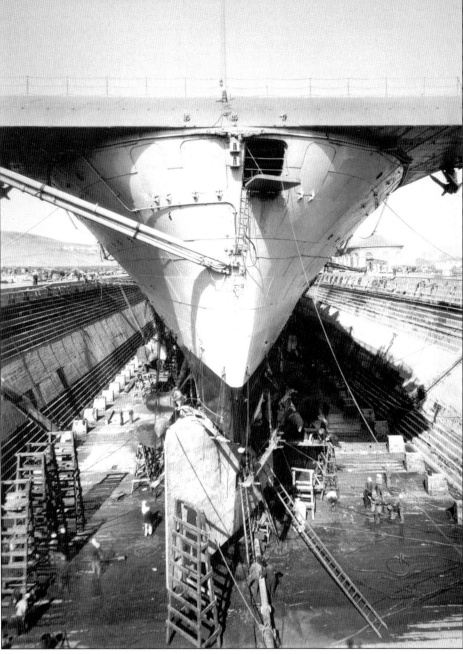

Following exercises off Southern California in May 1928, the *Saratoga* returned to San Francisco at the end of that month and went into dry dock at Hunter's Point Naval Shipyard for maintenance and repairs to her turbines. This view taken from the caisson of the dry dock on 13 June offers a close-up view of the carrier's stern and the aft end of the flight deck, including its sloping ramp. Spars for the stern life net are turned to the side. One of the eight ventilation doors at the main-deck level of the stern is open.

As viewed from her port side, the *Saratoga* is undergoing work in dry dock at Hunter's Point on 13 June 1928. No aircraft are present on the flight deck, as it was standard practice when going into dry dock for the carrier's air group to fly to a base on land. Prominent to the front of 8-inch gun turret number one is the crane, used for lowering seaplanes to the water or raising them back up to the flight deck, or for raising aircraft from a wharf to the flight deck.

USS *Saratoga* conducts a full-power trial run on 25 June 1928 off San Pedro, California. The carrier attained a speed of 33.42 knots and maintained an average speed of 33 knots during that day's trials, setting a new record for fastest ship in the world.

Saratoga is viewed from port during speed runs in late June 1928. The catwalk midway up the smokestack from the secondary conning station at the front of the stack to the aft primary battery control station was a feature that was not present on *Lexington*.

In a view taken two days after the preceding photo, looking forward over the forward 8-inch guns, the *Saratoga* is departing from dry dock at Hunter's Point. Details of the aircraft crane are visible, including the dark-colored kingpost and the girder from the top of the kingpost to the boom. Beyond the crane, bandsmen with instruments are standing on the deck. To the left and forward of the bandsmen is an open watertight hatch leading down to the main deck.

Saratoga's amidships area is seen from the starboard side during her second full-power trial run, 21 June 1928. Above the catwalk on the smokestack are two searchlight platforms. The *Saratoga* had searchlights on the starboard side of the smokestack only.

On 31 July 1928, *Saratoga* was once again in dry dock. In this view of the stern, workmen on planks suspended from the side of the ship are working on the hull. On the floor below the second-from-starboard propeller is the cone of the propeller.

This artistically superb view of the forward part of the USS *Saratoga* was taken during one of the ship's sojourns in dry dock at Hunter's Point Navy Shipyard in San Francisco in the late 1920s. The blunt shape of the bow is apparent. Riggings for staging planks are attached to fittings on the hull above the boot topping, the band of black paint running along the waterline of the ship. As water was pumped out of the dry dock, sailors and workmen on the planks would quickly scrape off the accumulations of marine growth from the hull before the growths could harden in the air. (National Museum of Naval Aviation)

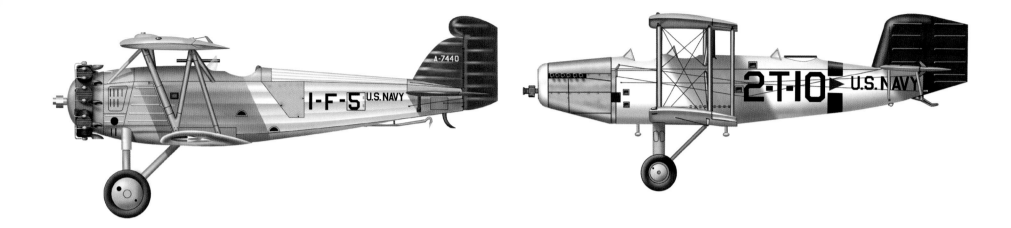

Boeing F2B-1 BuNo A7440 was assigned to VF-1B "High Hatters" in 1927. The F2B-1 had a top speed of 158 miles per hour, range of 315 miles, and carried one .50-caliber machine gun and one .30-caliber machine gun, or two .30s, plus 125 pounds of bombs.

In a circa-1929 view of the *Saratoga*'s flight deck facing aft, several Boeing F2B-1s are in the foreground, and behind them are Martin T4M-1 torpedo planes with markings for VT-2B. Torpedo Squadron 2B began transitioning to T4M-1s in August 1928. (San Diego Air and Space Museum)

This Martin T3M-2 was assigned to VT-2B on the *Saratoga* in 1928. The T3M-2 had a speed of 109 miles per hour, range of 635 miles, and was armed with a flex-mounted .30-caliber machine gun in the rear cockpit and one torpedo or bombs under the fuselage.

Maintaining the morale and physical fitness of the crew of any ship is important, and the crew of *Saratoga* had opportunities to test their physical skills and teamwork and have fun at the same time. Here, crewmen compete in a three-legged race around 1930. (San Diego Air and Space Museum)

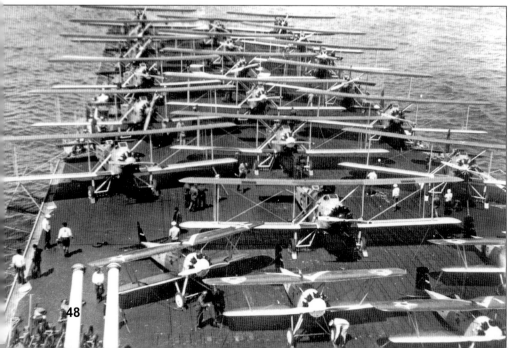

The *Saratoga* rides at anchor off Long Beach, California, in a photograph from 1929. A safety rail is installed across the front of the flight deck, and life nets are in the raised positions to the side of the flight deck. On the outboard edge of the platform of the 5-inch gun gallery below the aircraft crane, the three D-shaped platform extensions are in the lowered position. Farther aft, boat booms jut out from the side of the hull. Normally stowed against the hull, these booms were swung out when the ship was at anchor, enabling boats to be moored to them.

When *Saratoga* first crossed the equator on 23 January 1929, King Neptune and his court, shown here, presided over the time-honored ritual whereby so-called slimy polliwogs, who had never crossed the line before, were transformed into shellbacks. (San Diego Air and Space Museum)

During a crossing-the-line ceremony, shellbacks wielding paddles and water hoses give a group of slimy polliwogs a proper hazing as they walk a gauntlet. Even the ship's aircraft received an honor for crossing the equator: the right to wear a flying turtle insignia. (San Diego Air and Space Museum)

The angled, aft port leg of the foremast is adjacent to the rear corner of the island in this image from about 1929. Above the pilothouse, the radio-compass booth and the primary and secondary battery control stations are mounted on the forward leg of the formast.

Aircraft of VS-2B fly over the *Saratoga* on 25 September 1929. Eight-inch turrets three and four are visible in some detail. Aft of the smokestack, a short bipod mainmast supports the aft 8-inch guns' fire-control station and, above it, the aft 5-inch control station.

A Martin T4M-1 with a torpedo slung underneath its fuselage takes off from USS *Saratoga*. In the foreground is the forward starboard 5-inch/25-caliber Mk. 10 Mod. 1 antiaircraft gun gallery. The *Saratoga* carried 12 of these single-mount guns in four sponsons located on the main-deck level. Each mount weighed about two tons. The term "caliber" referred to the length of the gun barrel as a multiple of the diameter of the bore, so in the case of the 5-inch/25-caliber gun, the barrel was 125 inches long. (San Diego Air and Space Museum)

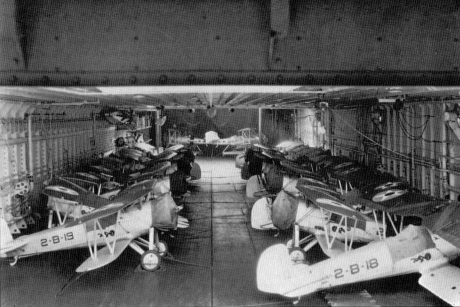

Boeing F3B-1 aircraft of FB-2B are stored in the hangar deck of the *Saratoga*. This squadron transitioned to F3B-1s in January 1929. Below the tarpaulins covering the cockpit openings is the squadron insignia, Felix the Cat running with a bomb with a lit fuse. (US Naval Institute)

Aircraft are lined up on the flight deck of *Saratoga* on 14 March 1929. At the center of the top platform of the foremast are the two forward 5-inch gun directors. On each side of the platform behind canvas windscreens are the forward 5-inch gun rangefinders. (National Museum of Naval Aviation)

Less than two years after his legendary solo flight from New York to Paris, Charles Lindbergh paid a visit to the *Saratoga* while she was deployed off the coast of Panama on 8 February 1929. Here, "Lucky Lindy" sits on a life net while visiting with officers. During his visit to the *Saratoga*, Lindbergh was inducted as an honorary member of VB-2B "Felix the Cat Squadron," and he flew the Boeing F3B-1 assigned to the commander of the squadron, Lt. Cdr. Arthur Davis. (San Diego Air and Space Museum)

In a 1929 aerial view, the *Saratoga*'s forward elevator is lowered. The wider, forward portion of the forward elevator well accommodated the elevator platform, while the narrower, aft part of the elevator well had two flaps which could be lowered, as seen here, to provide clearance for aircraft with long fuselages that extended beyond the elevator platform. When the flaps were in the raised position, they formed part of the flight deck, as did the forward elevator.

As viewed from the flight deck of *Saratoga*, a partially disassembled Loening amphibian aircraft rests on the hangar deck below. The code on the side of the fuselage indicates it was the 3rd aircraft of Utility Squadron 1B (VJ-1B. In May 1929 it is documented that Utility Squadron 1B brought aboard USS *Saratoga* two Loening amphibians. Visible to the lower left of the photo is the lowered platform of the elevator. (San Diego Air and Space Museum)

A prominent, new feature is present on the USS *Saratoga* in this photo: a highly visible vertical black stripe on the side of the smokestack. During the first year of the *Saratoga*'s active service, pilots of that carrier as well as *Saratoga*'s sister ship, USS *Lexington,* had difficulty discerning one carrier from the other, leading to landings on the wrong carrier. Hence, sometime between 15 March 1929 and 17 August 1929, a black vertical stripe was painted on each side of *Saratoga*'s smokestack as an identification aid. Around the same time, *Lexington* received a black band around the top of her smokestack.

In this aerial view of *Saratoga* taken around 1930, both the forward and aft elevators are lowered; the flap doors to the rear of the forward elevator are in their raised, or closed, position. Two circles that appear to have been recently painted are between the yellows stripes on the forward and aft parts of the mahogany-stained flight deck. The aft circle has spokes radiating from the center, while the forward circle lacks the spokes. The roofs of turret one and turret four have a dark colored longitudinal stripe. One of *Saratoga's* boats can be seen tied to the port boat boom.

Aircraft crowd the aft part of the flight deck of USS *Saratoga* around 1929. The fighter planes in the foreground, including some Boeing F2B-1s, are warming their engines preparatory to launching. In the late 1920s and early 1930s, *Saratoga's* squadrons often had several different types of fighters. In the background, longitudinal arrestor wires are visible; these were removed in 1929. To the right, life nets on the port side of the flight deck have been lowered to provide clearance to the wings of the aircraft. (National Museum of Naval Aviation)

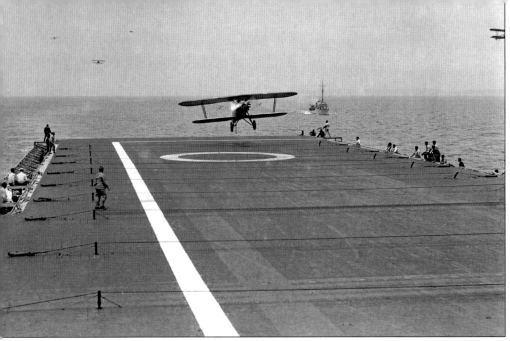

Arrestor hook extended to catch one of the lateral arrestors, an aircraft is about to touch down on *Saratoga* on 18 February 1930. The longitudinal arrestor wires have been removed. The landing signal officer (LSO) is at the aft port corner of the flight deck. (San Diego Air and Space Museum)

In early 1930 the *Saratoga* was ordered from Long Beach to the East Coast. Here, she is negotiating the Panama Canal's Pedro Miguel Locks on 4 March 1930. Visible on each side of the carrier are mules, electric locomotives on tracks, which towed ships through locks.

VT-2B flew Martin T4M-1 aircraft like this one from August 1930, when the type replaced the Great Lakes TG-1s flown by the squadron. Later the Martins were replaced by Naval Aircraft Factory TG-2 biplanes.

USS *Saratoga* makes her way through the Pedro Miguel Locks of the Panama Canal on 4 March 1930. After clearing the Panama Canal, the carrier would engage in Fleet Problems X and XI as a member of the Blue Force. These war games, conducted in the Caribbean, were important in the development of the Navy's carrier force, helping it to develop tactical doctrine and providing experience in scouting and attacking enemy naval forces at sea.

Following Fleet Problem XI, the *Saratoga* proceeded north to Portsmouth, Virginia, where she underwent maintenance at the naval yard, beginning on April 25. The *Saratoga* is depicted here departing from dry dock number four on 17 May 1930.

In early June 1930 the *Saratoga* departed from the East Coast of the United States, bound once again for California. She is shown here transiting locks in the Panama Canal on June 11. Two of the ventilation doors below the ramp of the flight deck are open. (Panama Canal Authority via Maritme Quest)

Sailors on the *Saratoga* caught this shark sometime around 1930. The snapshot offers a close-up view of a life net. To the left are the port kedge anchors and the *Saratoga* nameplate on the side of the support structure for the aft part of the flight deck. (San Diego Air and Space Museum)

Saratoga rides at anchor in San Francisco Bay on 18 August 1930. The carrier was in port to meet the Battle Fleet prior to fleet maneuvers the following week. Boats and barges cluster around the carrier, evidently ferrying personnel to shore. (U.S. Navy)

On 17 November 1930, USS *Saratoga* enters dry dock number two at the Navy Yard, Puget Sound (NYPS), Bremerton, Washington. This dry dock recently had been extended to accommodate ships of the size of *Saratoga,* and this new work is visible to the right. (Puget Sound Naval Shipyard)

In a view taken just shortly after the picture at left, the bow of the *Saratoga* is seen to be almost touching the end of the new extension of dry dock number two at NYPS. The *Saratoga* underwent maintenance and repairs at NYPS from 4 October to 2 December 1930.

USS *Saratoga* Standard Gray

Saratoga lies at anchor around 1930. She was still painted in a scheme of No. 5 Standard Navy Gray, with No. 20 Standard Deck Gray on the exposed steel decks, mahogany or maroon stain on the flight deck, and a vertical black stripe on the smokestack. *Saratoga* would wear the black stripe on her stack until World War II, although at various times the stripe was adorned with E awards or the ship's crowing cock emblem.

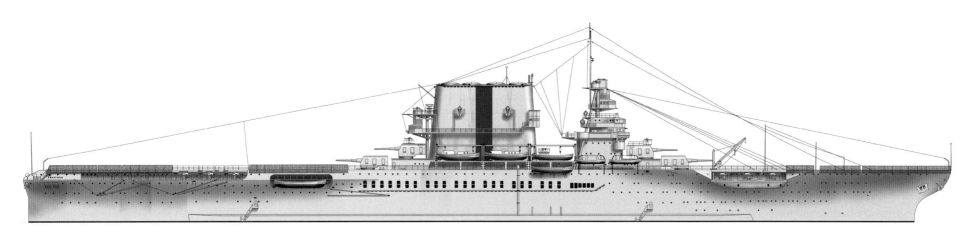

The *Saratoga* once again transited the Panama Canal on 23 March 1931 *en route* to war games in the Caribbean. It was difficult to con the ship through the tight confines of the locks from the pilothouse, offset to the starboard side of the ship, so the small booth shown in this photo was rigged over the vessel's longitudinal centerline. The ship's pilot occupied the booth, and from that vantage point he was better able to control the movements of the ship.

The mid and aft part of the flight deck of the *Saratoga* is viewed from the starboard side of the forward 5-inch battery director during the March 1931 transit of the Panama Canal. At the bottom, adjacent to the aft elevator, is a Vought O2U-1 Corsair fitted with floats. At the bottom left of the photo, the platform with two sailors standing on it on the front of the smokestack is the aviation control station, called Pri-Fly, below which is the secondary conning station. (San Diego Air and Space Museum)

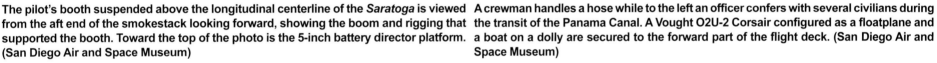

The pilot's booth suspended above the longitudinal centerline of the *Saratoga* is viewed from the aft end of the smokestack looking forward, showing the boom and rigging that supported the booth. Toward the top of the photo is the 5-inch battery director platform. (San Diego Air and Space Museum)

A crewman handles a hose while to the left an officer confers with several civilians during the transit of the Panama Canal. A Vought O2U-2 Corsair configured as a floatplane and a boat on a dolly are secured to the forward part of the flight deck. (San Diego Air and Space Museum)

Following exercises in the Caribbean in March and April 1931, *Saratoga* set out for San Diego, California, by way of the Panama Canal. The carrier is shown here negotiating the Culebra Cut in the canal on 5 April 1931. The pilot's control booth is again deployed.

The pilot's control booth is viewed from the front as *Saratoga* navigates the Gaillard Cut on 5 April 1931. To the right are aircraft of VS-2B with engine covers installed. In the foreground, a clear view is provided of the flap doors to the rear of the elevator.

The fronts of *Saratoga*'s island and smokestack are exhibited in detail from the forward port quarter in a photograph taken on the Panama Canal on 5 April 1931. The ship's bell hangs from the front of the navigation bridge, which wraps around the front and sides of the pilothouse. The next level above the pilothouse is the flag bridge, to the front of which is the 20-foot main-battery range finder, shown here turned to the side. Above the rangefinder is the radio-compass compartment; with one of its two front windows open. At the top is the main-battery director.

CAPITOL THEATRE Rome, N.Y.

Starting SUN., MON., TUE., FEB. 7, 8, 9

No Thrill EVER to Equal It!

HELL DIVERS

Do you want adventure? You'll risk your life in one daredevil flight after another! You'll conquer the dangers of sea and air. You'll fight your best pal and win the heart of the woman you want. You'll laugh and cry and feel your heart thumping when you see this magnificent spectacle!

Wallace **BEERY** Clark **GABLE**

Metro-Goldwyn-Mayer PICTURE

A year in the making. Laughs, Love, Action, Tragedy! Directed with cooperation of the U. S. Navy. 180 Aeroplanes take part in "HELL DIVERS". A new romance from the sky, in the Year's Biggest Picture! A thrilling entertainment for every man, woman and child! With hansome Clark Gable, lovable Wallace Beery, together now, in the picture hailed as the biggest of the Year. Bigger and Better than "Hells Angels." At popular Low Prices.

Released in 1932, the feature-length movie *The Hell Divers* featured much footage of flight operations filmed on USS *Saratoga*. The movie starred Wallace Beery and Clark Gable, who played rivals for the honors of best rear gunner in a dive-bomber squadron. Like most movies of the era, it was promoted through posters, which like this one, are highly collectible today.

Clark Gable, left, and Wallace Beery, right, sit with an unidentified man during a break on the set of *The Hell Divers.* Filming on the USS *Saratoga* took place in the summer of 1931. Several Navy pilots doubled for actors in flight scenes, including Lt. Jimmy Thach.

In a production still from *The Hell Divers,* Wallace Beery's character is being demoted for having been absent without leave. The location was on the flight deck between the rear of the island (right) and the front of the smokestack, in the background.

Crewmen of the *Saratoga* are seated under a cover rigged over the flight deck, apparently attending religious services. Details are visible of the structures at the rear of the island and mainmast and, passing through those structures, the aft port leg of the mainmast. (San Diego Air and Space Museum)

The number-three group of 5-inch/25-caliber weapons, located in the aft starboard sponson of the *Saratoga*, lets loose with a salvo during exercises off San Diego in early November 1931. These guns had a range of 27,400 feet at their maximum elevation of 85 degrees.

This profile represents the Curtiss F8C-4 Helldiver flown by Lt. Cdr. Arthur Radford, commander of VF-1B, in 1931. That squadron began acquiring its F8C-4s in August 1931. Curtiss F8C-4s were featured prominently in the movie The Hell Divers. The F8C-4 had a maximum speed of 137 miles per hour and a range of 455 miles. It was powered by the 450-horsepower Pratt & Whitney R-1340-4 radial engine. It mounted two .30-caliber machine guns in the nose and a flex-mounted .30-caliber machine gun in the observer's compartment.

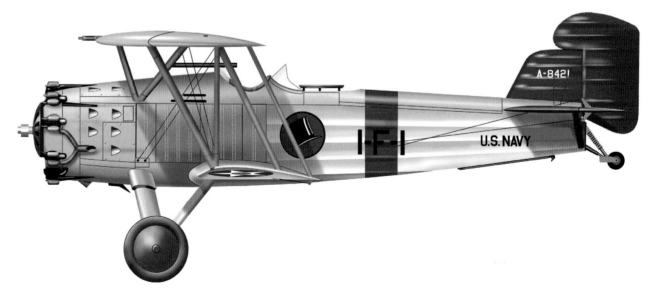

On 29 January 1932, Ensign J.W. Davison of VF-1B, flying a Boeing F4B, completed the 13,000th landing on USS *Saratoga*. Safe landings as well as the cumulative experience of making many landings were reasons for celebration on the navy's aircraft carriers.

A Vought O3U-2 Corsair assigned to VS-2B comes in for a landing on 2 March 1932. The vertical tail was White, and the bottom half of the cowl was Royal Red, signifying the third plane of the first section of the squadron.

A photographer in an aircraft took this view of USS *Saratoga* resting at anchor off San Pedro, California, on 28 March 1932. The photo gives a good idea of how the carrier's aircraft were parked on the flight deck. Several floatplanes, including what appears to be a Loening Amphibian on the port side of the deck, are parked sideways. Boat booms are extended to accommodate the small craft plying the waters around the ship.

A Loening OL-8A Amphibian catches an arrestor wire on *Saratoga* on 26 January 1932. The OL-8A was similar to the OL-8 but with arrestor gear installed. Over the following years, fewer and fewer seaplanes and amphibians would be found on U.S. carriers.

A Martin T4M-1, probably one assigned to VT-2B, touches down on the *Saratoga* on 6 January 1932. During that month, VT-2B augmented its complement of T4M-1s and Great Lakes TG-1s by acquiring seven Great Lakes TG-2 torpedo bombers.

On 2 March 1932 a Boeing F4B-2 of VF-6B "Felix the Cat Squadron" takes off from the *Saratoga*. This squadron had been redesignated from VF-6B to VB-2B in July 1928 but was redesignated VF-6B in July 1930, and it transitioned to F4B-2s in February 1931.

On USS *Saratoga*'s landing number 13,716 on 11 March 1932, a Vought O3U-2 flown by Lt. (j.g.) Aldeman went out of control after crossing the ramp, crashing into the aft port 5-inch gun group. The propeller hasn't completely stopped spinning yet.

The USS *Saratoga* is at anchor off San Diego, California, in April 1932. The yellow guide lines on the flight deck are highly visible in this photograph. Faintly visible on the aft end of her flight deck is the abbreviation "SARA," which has been painted as an aid for returning pilots to identify the ship, particularly when she was operating near her sister ship, USS *Lexington*. On top of the mainmast, the two directors and the two altimeters in the 5-inch gun battery control station have light-colored protective covers over them.

Civilians inspect the aircraft on the *Saratoga* during Visitors' Day at Long Beach, California, in April 1932. In the foreground are Boeing F4B2s of VF-6B; the one at the lower right has the side number 6-F-9. In the background is USS *Lexington.* (National Museum of Naval Aviation)

A *Saratoga* crewman took this snapshot of the starboard side of the carrier at Coronado, California, in April 1932. At the time, the carrier was sitting low in the water, as the black boot topping at the waterline is barely visible. The 5-inch guns have fitted covers on them. (National Museum of Naval Aviation)

In a late-April 1932 aerial photograph of the *Saratoga*, the carrier's air group is parked from amidships to the front of the flight deck. Aircraft are parked in no particular order in reference to their type. It was the job of the flight deck officer to see to the spotting of the aircraft on deck once all of the aircraft had landed. The planes were parked forward on the flight deck during landing operations and then pushed aft, with care taken to properly spot the aircraft in readiness, insofar as was possible, for the next mission.

The Loening XO2L-1 is undergoing carrier qualification on 12 October 1932. The XO2L-1 was an improved version of the Loening OL-6 amphibian. Only one example of the XO2L-1, BuNo A8525, was produced, and it did not go into production. (San Diego Air and Space Museum)

Flight-deck airplane handlers known as airdales rush out to assist Great Lakes TG-2 BuNo A8711, which has careened into a 5-inch gun gallery while landing on 28 November 1932. Some airdales are on the wing to help stabilize the plane.

Looking aft on the port wing of the navigating bridge of the *Saratoga* was a board with three lights by which the flight-deck control officer signaled aircraft preparing to take off to stop, exercise caution, or go. Seaman 2nd Class R. A. Scherer is the crewman.

To the left on the deck of the *Saratoga* on 28 January 1933 is Grumman XSF-1 BuNo A8940, the prototype of the SF-1 scout plane. To the right is Vought SU-1 Corsair BuNo A9063 with markings for VF-1B. The carrier was *en route* to Hawaii for war games.

Aircraft are parked aft of the erected palisades on *Saratoga*, 28 January 1933. The palisades helped alleviate the effects of wind on the lightweight, fragile biplanes. Each stake of the palisade was hinged and equipped with a brace on the forward side.

A Boeing F4B-3 of VF-1B has the Lemon Yellow cowl and fuselage band, indicating the leader of the sixth section. A white "E" for excellence award is on the fuselage below the cockpit windshield Armament comprised two .30-cal or one .30- and one 0.50-caliber machine guns. Maximum speed was 189 miles per hour, and range was 570 miles.

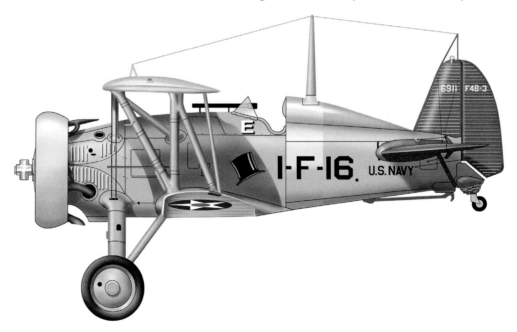

Lieutenant (j.g.) Gaines of VF-1B crashed F4B-3 side number 1-F-3 into the barrier on USS Saratoga on 9 February 1933. Hitting the barrier wires was the last chance to stop a landing aircraft that had missed all of the arrestor wires. Often the results were like this.

Boeing F4B-4 BuNo A9044 of VF-6B "Felix the Cat Squadron" touches down on USS Saratoga on 6 February 1933. In the right background is a windscreen designed to protect the landing signal officer (LSO) at the aft port corner of the flight deck from gusts.

Boeing F4B-4 side number I-F-5 served on Saratoga from 1933 to 1934. The F4B-4's armament comprised two .30-cal or one .30- and one 0.50-caliber machine guns and 500 pounds of bombs. Maximum speed was 189 miles per hour and range was 570 miles.

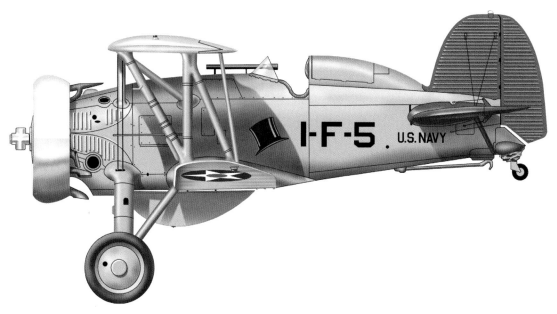

The port side of *Saratoga*'s island is viewed looking upward in February 1933. To the lower left is the port wing of the navigating bridge, including the flight-deck control officer's light-signal board. The frames supporting the fire-control stations are visible.

Airdales on *Saratoga*'s flight deck watch Boeing F4B-4s on the forward elevator. The plane to the left bears markings for VF-6B and a black chevron indicating Section 4 of the squadron, while the other plane's chevron is white, for Section 2. (US Naval Institute)

The forward part of the flight deck of the *Saratoga* is viewed from the bridge in a photograph dating from around the early 1930s. On top of 8-inch turret two is a twin .50-caliber machine gun mount with the machine guns dismounted. A similar twin .50-caliber machine gun mount was on top of turret three during this period. The mount atop turret two was removed during a 1933–34 overhaul of the carrier, but the twin .50-caliber mount on turret three was not removed at that time. (San Diego Air and Space Museum)

This view of the smokestack and aft 8-inch/55-caliber gun turrets of *Saratoga* was taken while the carrier was anchored off Honolulu on 2 February 1933. A close examination of the image reveals a twin .50-caliber machine gun mount on the roof of turret three.

Landing number 16,130 on USS *Saratoga* on 9 February 1933 concluded with the plane, a Boeing F4B, side number 1-F-17, crashing into the barrier wires. The pilot survived. As the second plane in its section, it had a Lemon Yellow top half of the engine face plate.

Majestic cloud formations tower over the Pacific Ocean in an early 1930s view forward from aft of 8-inch turret four. Adjacent to the right 8-inch gun on each of the 8-inch turrets is a sight hood for the trainer, who controlled the traverse of the mount when the main-battery director was not exercising automatic control over the mount. A similar hood on the left side of the face plate of the turret was provided for the pointer's sight. The pointer controlled the elevation of the piece when the mount was not under automatic control. (National Museum of Naval Aviation)

73

A photographer aboard USS *Lexington* shot this portrait of sister ship USS *Saratoga* at anchor in San Francisco Harbor in early 1933. During war games in mid-February, aircraft from the *Saratoga* conducted a mock air raid on the city of San Francisco.

By early 1933, *Saratoga* had undergone a refitting in which the radio-compass booth was removed from below the main-battery director to make room for a flag plot above the pilothouse. The main-battery rangefinder was moved to atop the flag plot. (National Museum of Naval Aviation)

For the benefit of a Paramount newsreel team, on 28 August 1933, crewmen on the flight deck of *Saratoga* were arrayed to spell NRA, the acronym for the National Recovery Administration, part of the Franklin Roosevelt administration's "New Deal." Also in view is Goodyear blimp *Volunteer.*

Saratoga stars on the silver screen

In addition to her more serious tasks, *Saratoga* attracted the Hollywood limelight on two occasions in the 1930s. In 1931 Wallace Beery and Clark Gable walked her decks during the filming of the drama *Hell Divers*. A drama about Navy aviators set on the ship, *Hell Divers* featured a back story of the love interests of the leading men and their leading ladies (Marjorie Rambeau and Dorothy Jordan). The movie cameras returned two years later to make Joe E. Brown's *Son of a Sailor*, an almost pure comedy, with only a thin dramatic back story.

Today, *Hell Divers* offers a rare glimpse of carrier operations during the pre-WWII era, showcasing the ship, her aircraft, and flight operations. It is also a reminder that at the time *Saratoga* boasted such cutting-edge naval aviation technology that black bars were inserted at the bottom of some film frames to block close-ups of the arresting hooks and wires.

In *Son of a Sailor,* Brown costared with Thelma Todd and Jean Muir. Released in 1933, this film focuses on the comedic talents of the cast, and *Saratoga,* at that time home ported in San Diego, was a convenient tableau for the players. The cast and crew from Warner Brothers boarded on 30 August, 1933, and wrapped up shooting on Saturday, 2 September. The movie was in theaters by 30 November of the same year.

It was not unusual during this era for the Navy to authorize Hollywood productions aboard its vessels. While recruitment was not a problem for the Navy during the depression-wrought 1930s, there was a keen desire to show the public in a positive way what their tax dollars were buying.

In late August 1933 the *Saratoga* again was used as a location film set when a Warner Brothers crew filmed some scenes for the feature-length comedy *Son of a Sailor.* The film crew was on the ship for four days, wrapping up work there on 2 September.

The star of *Son of a Sailor,* Joe E. Brown, reclines on a locker-room bench in a production still from the movie. The navy was liberal in allowing movie companies to film on its ships, since these movies were useful tools in recruiting and public relations.

This production still from *Son of a Sailor* shows star Joe E. Brown after knocking-out his opponent in a boxing match. This scene was filmed on the flight deck of the *Saratoga.* Behind the sailors to the right is what appears to be a leg of one of the ship's masts.

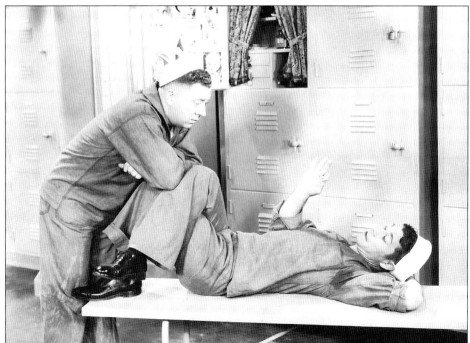

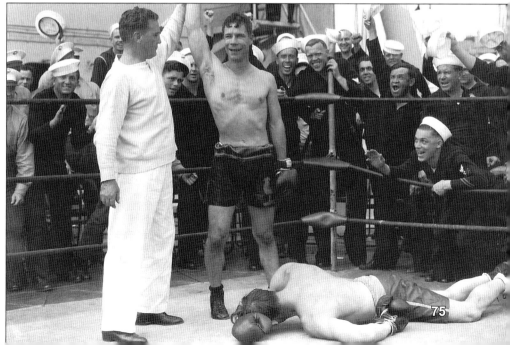

75

The *Saratoga* is docked at an unidentified port, probably in the early 1930s. Judging from the evergreen trees visible above the aft part of the flight deck, the scene was likely the Navy Yard, Puget Sound, during one of *Saratoga*'s visits for maintenance and modifications. What appear to be tarpaulins are hanging in the boat bay. Two barges are stored under the davits alongside the smokestack. In addition, most of the ventilator doors on the hull below the smokestack are open.

A Vought Corsair prepares for takeoff. The structure atop 8-inch turret two is a splinter shield for two single-mounted .50-caliber machine guns installed during the December 1933-February 1934 overhaul at NYPS. Eventually the shield would be removed because it interfered with the forward vision of personnel in the conning tower: the structure with vision slits located below the navigating bridge. The radio-compass booth below the forward main-battery control station had been removed in 1933. (San Diego Air and Space Museum)

Beginning in 1928, there was an intense concentration of U.S Naval might, including the *Saratoga* and her sister ship *Lexington* (CV-2), on the American West Coast, and from 1930, the U.S. Battle Fleet was based there as well. On 3 November 1933, the White House announced that the U.S. fleet would visit the East Coast in 1934. In time, the sailing date of 9 April 1934 was announced, and on that day the 104 ships and 46,000 men under command of Admiral David Sellers set off for the East Coast. *En route* to Panama, the force was divided into two mock fleets, and war games were conducted along the way, ending with a simulated attack on the U.S. Army defenders of Panama. After the games were concluded, it took 47 hours for the armada to pass through the Panama Canal. Once in the Caribbean, further fleet exercises ensued, until finally on 25 May 1934 the fleet, including *Saratoga,* swung toward New York, arriving off New York City enveloped in fog in the dark morning hours of 31 May.

With the fog lifted, and the bright sun in the sky, the fleet formed a column and passed before President Franklin D. Roosevelt, who reviewed the fleet from the deck of the cruiser *Indianapolis* (CA-35). Admiral Sellers' flagship, the battleship *Pennsylvania* (BB-38), led the column, followed by *Saratoga,* with her two destroyer plane guards, and then the *Lexington.* After passing the *Indianapolis, Saratoga* and *Lexington* turned into the wind and launched a combined 185 aircraft. Once the air operations were complete, both carriers tied up to Pier 90 in New York City, where they would remain, open to the public for tours, until 19 June.

Boeing F4B-4s are being spotted for takeoff over the *Saratoga*'s stern on 17 May 1934. Naval planners thought that such flexibility in launching and recovering planes could be a critical advantage if part of the flight deck was rendered unusable in an attack.

Because the Lexington-class carriers had turbo-electric power for their propellers, they were able to proceed at equivalent speeds aft and forward. In part because of this ability to navigate stern-first, it was deemed expedient to make provisions on these carriers to conduct aircraft launches over the stern and arrested landings over the bow. Here, an F4B takes off over the stern while the *Saratoga* is making 15 knots astern on 17 May 1934.

On 23 June 1934, five days after she left New York's Pier 90, *Saratoga* entered Norfolk harbor and Marc Mitscher returned to the ship's company, now serving as Executive Officer under her captain, Kenneth Whiting. *Saratoga* passed westwardly through the Panama Canal on 23 October.

Almost a year later, *Saratoga* was bound for Hawaii in yet another exercise, and while there it was announced that she would be receiving a new Captain, William F. Halsey. Halsey took command on 3 July 1935, after *Saratoga* had returned to the U.S. West Coast. Halsey remained *Saratoga's* captain through her appearance at the grand opening of the Golden Gate Bridge on 28 May 1937. Then on 8 June Captain John Towers replaced Halsey as *Saratoga's* captain, but as had been the case with Mitscher, this would not be the last time Halsey's career touched *Saratoga*.

While in 1936, the flight deck of *Lexington* had been widened, and a similar change was planned for *Saratoga*, along with an increase in her antiaircraft defense, similar to the upgrade in armament *Lexington* received in 1935. In actual fact, such improvements were not made to *Saratoga* contemporaneously. Funding for the *Saratoga's* improvements was finally appropriated by Congress in June 1939, but by that time, war had broken out in Europe. The Navy was reluctant to tie up *Saratoga* for the 11-month yard period needed to accomplish all the planned improvements, so many of the improvements to *Saratoga* were cancelled. Finally, however, on 6 January 1941, she entered Puget Sound Navy Yard to have widened bow flight deck and augmented antiaircraft battery fitted during a 120-day yard period.

Saratoga, right, and Lexington, left, are viewed from the front during their 1934 visit to New York City. For this occasion, the Saratoga had a nameplate affixed to her bow. Both carriers' aircraft remained onboard during this sojourn, allowing visitors to view them.

In late May and early June 1934 the USS *Saratoga* visited New York Harbor. She is seen here on the left, with her sister ship, USS *Lexington,* to the right. The visit to New York also included a review of the Naval force by President Franklin D. Roosevelt. (US Naval Institute)

Seen in this view of the *Lexington* from the *Saratoga,* visitors throng to visit the carriers docked in New York City in 1934. These formidable examples of military might served to remind Americans suffering through the depths of the Great Depression that the United States remained a great power. (US Naval Institute)

Saratoga is underway in late May 1935 *en route* to a presidential review at New York. Faintly visible on the vertical stripe on the smokestack is an insignia of a crowing cock, which had been symbol of the Navy's ships named *Saratoga* since the War of 1812.

Carriers such as the *Saratoga* often supplied fuel and supplies to their escorts in an operation called underway replenishment, or UNREP. This view of *Saratoga* conducting an UNREP also offers a close-up view of the forward starboard 5-inch gun group.

This Curtiss BFC-2 served with VB-3, formerly VB-2B, in 1937. The letter C by the cockpit was an award for communications. The BFC-2 had a top speed of 202 miles per hour and a range of 559 miles. The plane was armed with two .30-caliber machine guns.

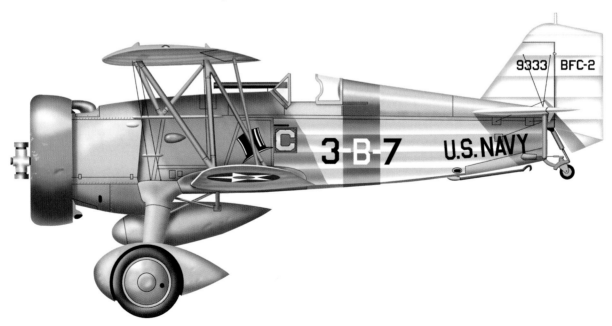

Anchored off San Francisco, the USS *Saratoga* is decked-out in full dress in celebration of George Washington's Birthday, 22 February 1935. The ship's air group has disembarked from the carrier, and a boat is stored at the front end of the flight deck.

The crowing cock insignia that had been present on the smokestack in 1934 had been painted over when *Saratoga* was photographed at San Diego in April 1935. The dark areas on the hull are shadows cast by the sponsons and the curvature of the hull.

Perched on a plank suspended from the smokestack, two crewmen clean and paint the stack sometime in the 1930s. Whether at sea or in port or dry dock, maintenance on the painted finishes of the *Saratoga* was a task that never ended. To the top right is the lower part of the secondary conning station. Below are boat davits and, at the bottom of the photograph, the aft part of one of the carrier's barges.

The *Saratoga* is seen from overhead as she sits in dry dock at the Navy Yard, Puget Sound, Bremerton, Washington, receiving her traditional winter maintenance, modifications, and repairs on 21 November 1935. At the bottom of the photo, "SARA" is visible just forward of the ramp at the rear of the flight deck. Next to the smokestack, the aft elevator is lowered, exposing the white forward bulkhead of the elevator well.

The USS *Saratoga* had completed her winter cycle of upkeep and modifications at the Navy Yard, Puget Sound, when she was photographed on 13 January 1936. The following day, the carrier would depart for Long Beach, California. One of the more noticeable modifications the carrier received during this period at the yard was a redesigned navigating bridge. Previously, the top edge of the center of the front of the bridge had been lower than the tops of the wings of the bridge. Now, the forward face of the bridge had a uniform height from side to side and included a wind deflector. (Puget Sound Naval Shipyard)

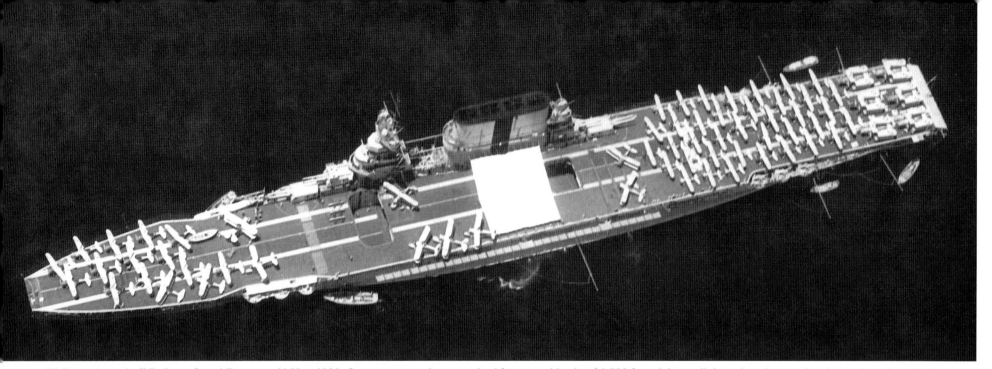

While anchored off Balboa, Canal Zone, on 11 May 1936, *Saratoga* was photographed from an altitude of 1,500 feet. A large, light-colored cover has been rigged amidships, and a variety of aircraft types, including several floatplanes, are parked on the flight deck.

A Neptune party is in full swing as the *Saratoga* once again marks a crossing of the equator. Crewmen who have already earned shellback status enjoy the proceedings as Polliwogs walk the gauntlet on the flight deck. (National Archives via Rob Stern)

Vought SBU-1 BuNo A9772 served as a utility aircraft with VB-3 on *Saratoga* in 1937. The SBU-1 had a maximum speed of 205 miles per hour, a range of 548 miles, a fixed, forward-firing .30-caliber machine gun, and a .30-caliber machine gun in the aft cockpit.

USS *Saratoga* 1936 Plans

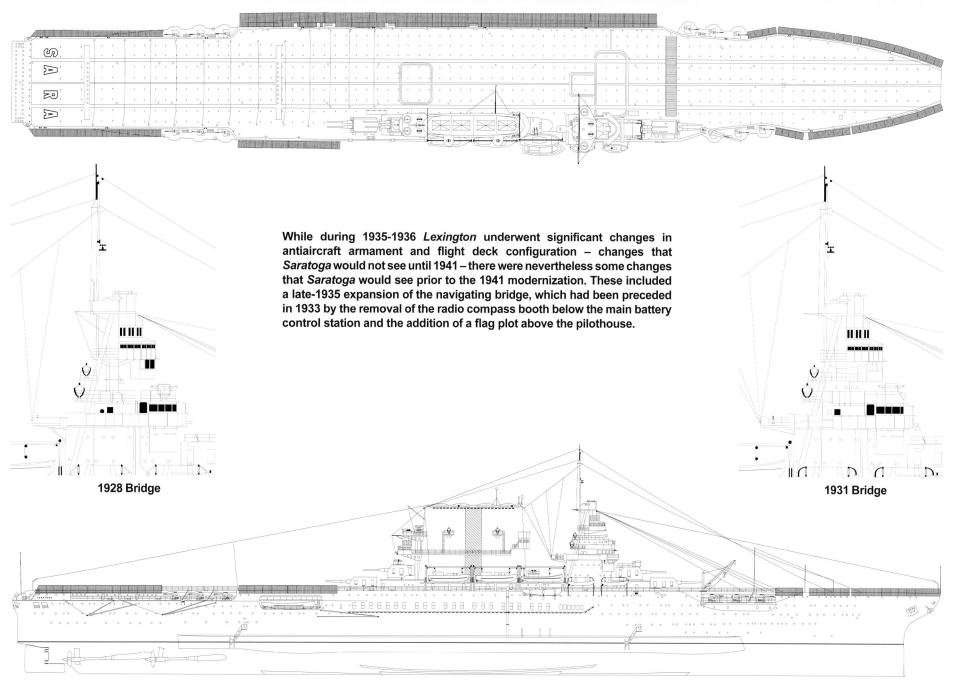

While during 1935-1936 *Lexington* underwent significant changes in antiaircraft armament and flight deck configuration – changes that *Saratoga* would not see until 1941 – there were nevertheless some changes that *Saratoga* would see prior to the 1941 modernization. These included a late-1935 expansion of the navigating bridge, which had been preceded in 1933 by the removal of the radio compass booth below the main battery control station and the addition of a flag plot above the pilothouse.

1928 Bridge

1931 Bridge

Her flight deck packed with aircraft, USS *Saratoga* rides at anchor at Coronado Roads, off San Diego, on 26 February 1937. Prominently displayed on the vertical black stripe on the smokestack is a large capital E, representing the much-coveted annual award for excellence in the engineering department. The commander of the *Saratoga* at this time was Capt. William F. Halsey Jr., later to gain fame as one of the great admirals of World War II. (National Museum of Naval Aviation)

CV-3 *Saratoga* General Data

The *Saratoga* is observed from aft at Coronado Roads, California, on 26 February 1937. In the days before all of a U.S. Navy aircraft carrier's aircraft were equipped with folding wings, it was necessary to carefully orchestrate the spotting of planes on the flight deck. The roofs of the 8-inch turrets had been painted a dark color, most likely during the recent visit to the Navy Yard, Puget Sound. The smokestack cap was painted black. (National Museum of Naval Aviation)

Dimensions

Length, overall, as built:	888 feet 6 inches
Length, overall, 1944:	910 feet 1¾ inch
Length between perpendiculars:	850 feet
Maximum beam:	130 feet 1½ inch
Waterline beam, as built:	105 feet 5¼ inches
Waterline beam, post-1942:	111 feet 9 inches
Flight Deck dimensions, 1941:	866 feet 2 inches x 105 feet 11¼ inches
Hangar Deck:	393 feet x 68 feet x 20 feet
Draft, max, as built:	31 feet 10⅜ inches
Draft, max, 1943:	32 feet 6 inches
Draft, max, 1945:	36 feet 3 inches
Displacement, light:	34,067 tons
Displacement, standard:	41,187 tons
Displacement, full load, 1936:	43,054 tons
Displacement, full load, 1942:	47,879 tons
Displacement, full load, 1944:	48,550 tons

Armor

Main belt:	5 feet 7 inches
Flight and Hangar deck:	0 inches
Protective deck:	2 inches
Conning tower:	80-lb STS

Ship's complement, as designed:	148 officers, 1,500 men
Ship's complement, 1938:	79 officers, 1,354 men
Ship's complement, 1944:	121 officers; 2,021 men
Air wing, 1944:	163 officers; 761 men

Armament

1927:	8 8-inch/55 caliber; 12 5-inch/25 caliber
1941:	8 8-inch/55 caliber; 12 5-inch/25 caliber; 5 3-inch/50 caliber; 8 .50 caliber BMG
1942:	16 5-inch/38 caliber; 36 1.1-inch in 9 quad mounts; 32 20mm
1943:	16 5-inch/38 caliber; 36 40mm in 9 quad mounts; 52 20mm
1944:	16 5-inch/38 caliber; 96 40mm in 24 quad mounts; 16 20mm
1945:	16 5-inch/38 caliber; 100 40mm in 25 quad mounts; 16 20mm

Air Wing:	Varies, 70 to 87 aircraft
Aviation fuel:	137,450 gallons

Aviation Munitions allowance, May 1942: 700 x 100-lb bombs; 550 x 100-lb incendiary bombs; 200 x 325-lb depth bombs; 700 x 500-lb bombs; 300 x 1,000-lb bombs; 54 x 1,600-lb bombs.

On 4 October 1937, USS *Saratoga* was once again at the Navy Yard, Puget Sound. The ship's paint appears to be fresh, and the E award is faintly visible on the smokestack. Although the *Saratoga* still retained the original narrow front end of the flight deck, the previous year the flight deck aboard her sister ship, USS *Lexington,* had been widened considerably. The difference made it much easier for pilots to distinguish the sister carriers when returning to their ships. (Puget Sound Naval Shipyard)

The *Saratoga* is viewed from her starboard side at the Navy Yard, Puget Sound, on 4 October 1937. While USS *Lexington* had undergone considerable upgrades in 1935 and 1936, including but not limited to the widened front of the flight deck, the addition of new antiaircraft weapons and sponsons, and the installation of a machine gun and searchlight platform around the smokestack, such modifications to the *Saratoga* had been deferred. (Puget Sound Naval Shipyard)

Operations are underway on *Saratoga* to salvage Vought SBU-1 BuNo 9831, which had gone into the drink. A hoist line is secured to the propeller shaft. Below the upper wing are flotation bags, which apparently had deployed as intended when the plane crashed. (Naval History and Heritage Command)

As the salvage of SBU-1 BuNo 9831 proceeds, a hoist line from the *Saratoga*'s aircraft crane attached to a pole inserted in the lifting tube toward the rear of the fuselage will be used to raise the tail of the plane so the aircraft can be set down on its landing gear. (Naval History and Heritage Command)

A new breed of U.S. Navy dive bomber, the monoplane Vought SB2U-1 Vindicator, such as this example on the flight deck of *Saratoga* in 1938, entered service with that carrier in VB-3, beginning in December 1937. It carried a two-man crew of pilot and gunner. (Naval History and Heritage Command)

Also entering service on the *Saratoga* in late 1937 was the Douglas TBD-1 Devastator. In October 1937, VT-3 began transitioning to this monoplane torpedo bomber. Here a TBD-1 has just completed the 38,000th landing on *Saratoga* on 21 January 1938. (National Archives)

A Douglas TBD-1 takes off from USS *Saratoga* on 21 January 1938. The TBD-1 was considered quite sophisticated at the time it entered the service, but events and technical developments would render the plane obsolescent by the beginning of World War II.

Six TBD-1 Devastators of VT-3 are secured to the flight deck of USS *Saratoga* on 26 January 1938. These aircraft boasted fully enclosed cockpits with streamlined canopies for the three-man crew, retractable landing gear, and folding wings to facilitate storage.

This Douglas TBD-1 served with VT-3 on *Saratoga*. The TBD-1 had a maximum speed of 206 miles per hour and range of 535 miles, and mounted one fixed and one flex-mount .30-caliber machine gun as well as a Mk. 13 torpedo or 1,000 pounds of bombs.

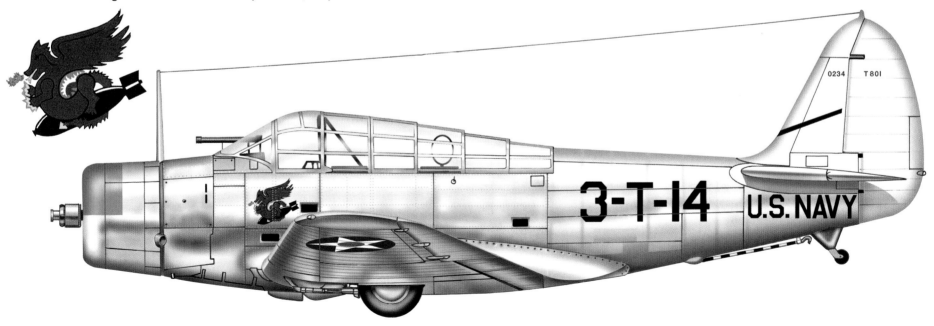

Vought SB2U-1 Vindicators of VB-3 are parked on the flight deck of USS *Saratoga* on 8 February 1938. As seen on 3-B-5 in the background, when opened, the two aft sections of the rear canopy slid forward underneath the forward, fixed section of the rear canopy.

SB2U-1 BuNo 0727 of VB-3 has landed on *Saratoga* on 8 February 1938; its tailhook is free of the arrestor wire. To the left, a member of the Air Department motions the pilot forward. The flight deck officer was in charge of moving planes around on that deck.

SB2U-1 BuNo 0757 served with VB-3 "High Hatters" on *Saratoga*. The SB2U-1 had a top speed of 249 miles per hour, a range of 1,300 miles with auxiliary tank, and was armed with one fixed and one flex-mounted .30-caliber machine gun, plus bombs.

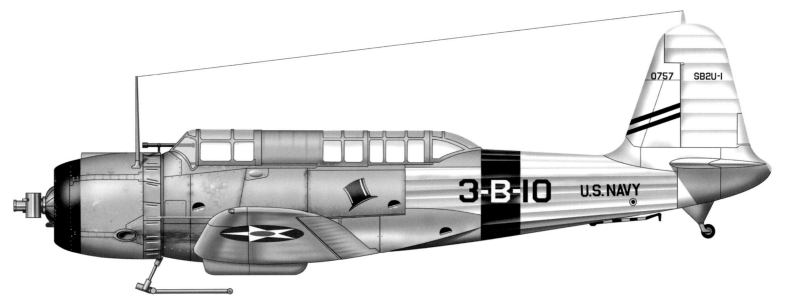

USS *Saratoga* rides at anchor, her air group disembarked, in an unidentified harbor around the late 1930s. The slanted white hash mark below the "E" engineering award on the smokestack indicated that the *Saratoga* had once again won that annual award. (Patty Anderson)

Grumman F3F-1 BuNo 0260, assigned to VF-3 on *Saratoga*, appears in its circa-1938 colors and markings. The F3F-1 was armed with one .30-caliber and one .50-caliber machine gun. It had a maximum speed of 231 miles per hour and a range of approximately 950 miles.

In a snapshot of sailors dressed in their whites, perhaps taken on a boat bound for shore liberty, the slanted white hash mark under the "E" engineering award on the port side of *Saratoga* is visible. Liberty was an occasion every sailor looked forward to. (San Diego Air and Space Museum)

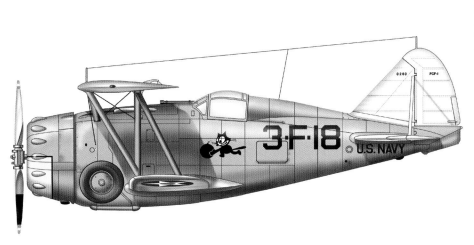

USS *Saratoga* is docked at the Navy Yard, Puget Sound, on 9 January 1940. The "E" and hashmark below it are still present on the vertical black stripe on the smokestack. Ten days later, the carrier would enter dry dock number two for maintenance, repairs, and modifications. The 5-inch/25-caliber gun mounts have covers over all but their barrels. The carrier's upper works still lack radar antennas; these would not appear until the following year.

A photographer on USS *Lexington* (CV-2) photographed her sister ship, USS *Saratoga*, launching aircraft while en route from California to Hawaii during during Fleet Problem XXI on 4 April 1940. In the foreground is the heavy cruiser USS *Portland* (CA-33).

A photographer in the rear seat of a Douglas TBD that had just taken off from USS *Saratoga* snapped this photograph of the carrier, probably sometime between December 1941 and early January 1942. Other TBDs on the flight deck are preparing to take off. A significant modification to the *Saratoga* is evident: the forward end of the flight deck had been widened at the Navy Yard, Puget Sound, in the first four months of 1941. New sponsons for 3-inch antiaircraft guns also had been added to the side of the hull near the bow. In November 1941, these 3-inch guns were replaced by quadruple 1.1-inch automatic guns.

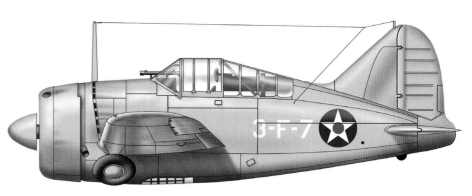

The bow and island of USS *Saratoga* are visible above a forest of scaffolding at the Navy Yard, Puget Sound, Bremerton, Washington, in April 1941. The widened bow is evident, and the new forward starboard sponson for a 3-inch gun is faintly visible near the bow.

Fighter Squadron 3 flew Brewster F2A-2 Buffalos from October 1940 to September 1941, including this example. It had a top speed of 344 miles per hour and range of 1,670 miles. Armament consisted of four .50-caliber machine guns and two 100-pound bombs.

This Curtiss SBC-4 served with VB-4 aboard USS *Saratoga* in 1941. This aircraft had a maximum speed of 234 miles per hour and a range of 405 miles. It was armed with one fixed and one flex-mounted .30-caliber machine gun and up to 1,000 pounds of bombs. Aircraft lettering was changed to white due to *Saratoga* being assigned to Carrier Division One.

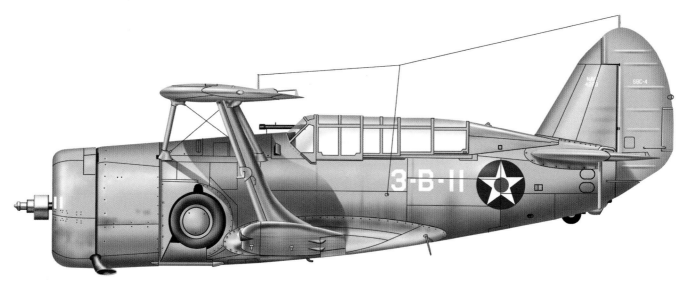

Grumman F4F-3 Wildcat BuNo 3982 of the 3rd Section of VF-3 is on the elevator of USS *Saratoga* in early October 1941. At that time, its pilot was Ens. Gayle Hermann. Other F4F-3s are secured to the flight deck to prevent the wind from whipping them around.

A member of the flight-deck crew signals by hand as a Gruman F4F-3 Wildcat of VF-3 runs up its engine on *Saratoga* around October 1941. This squadron had flown Brewster Buffalos for less than a year when it transitioned to the F4F-3 in September 1941.

A Grumman F4F-3 of VF-3 in 1941 has a Light Gray paint scheme. This model of the Grumman Wildcat had a maximum speed of 331 miles per hour, range of 845 miles, and armament of four wing-mounted .50-caliber machine guns and two 100-pound bombs.

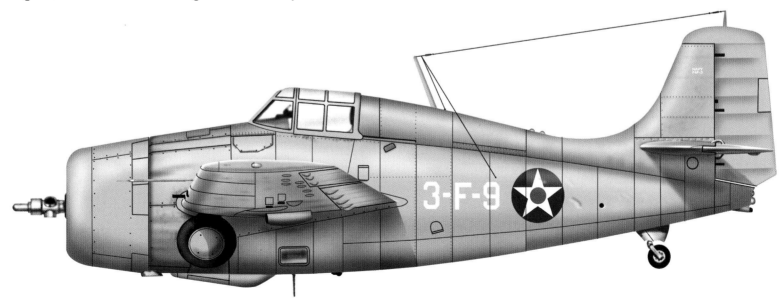

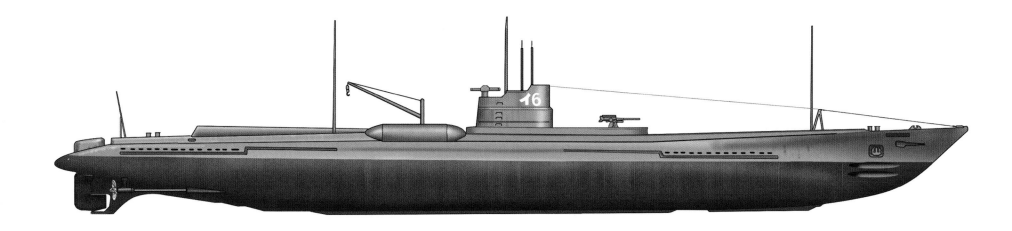

On 11 January 1942, *Saratoga* was operating with Task Force 14 northwest of Pearl Harbor when a Japanese submarine, I-6, scored a torpedo hit on the carrier. *Saratoga* managed to make it back to Pearl Harbor, receiving temporary repairs there.

A photograph taken in dry dock at Pearl Harbor on 16 January 1942 documents the torpedo damage to the port side of the hull between frames 100 and 111, which resulted in flooding to boiler rooms 8, 10, and 12 and to three void tanks in the stability blister.

As viewed looking down from the top of dry dock two at Pearl Harbor, the workmen on the floor of the dry dock provide a sense of the size of the torpedo breach in the port side of *Saratoga*. The ship received temporary repairs at Pearl through the rest of January.

98

Saratoga goes to war

Repairs as well as installation of improved antiaircraft defenses for *Saratoga* were completed at Puget Sound by 2 December 1941, and two days later she got underway, bound for San Diego, where she was to embark her air group, as well as Marine Fighting Squadron (VMF) 221. *Saratoga* entered the San Diego bay and tied up at North Island, the Naval Air Station, at 11:32 hours, 7 December 1941. Twelve minutes later word was passed over the ship's speakers that Pearl Harbor had been attacked. Working through the night, *Saratoga's* crew and shipyard workers had her provisioned, and 103 aircraft aboard in incredible time, and at 0958 hours on 8 December she was underway, bound for Pearl Harbor.

Just over a month later, on 11 January 1942, *Saratoga* was struck by a torpedo launched by the Japanese submarine I-6. This would not be *Saratoga's* only encounter with a Japanese torpedo. The strike forced *Saratoga* to return first to Pearl Harbor, and then to Puget Sound, for repairs and modernization. One of the most visible changes made to the ship was the removal of her four two-gun 8-inch/55 turrets. If nothing else, Pearl Harbor had proven the unlikelihood of a carrier being involved in a surface action. In the place of the big guns, new dual-purpose 5-inch, 38 caliber twin mounts were installed, substantially bolstering her antiaircraft defenses. But the 8-inch turrets were not discarded, rather, they were given to the army, who installed them as coastal defense batteries Brodie and Salt Lake in Hawaii, where they remained until they were scrapped in 1948.

During repairs at Pearl Harbor in early 1942, *Saratoga*'s 8-inch turrets were removed and transferred to the army for coastal defense. This photo shows one of *Lexington's* 8-inch turrets being removed, since no photos of the removal of *Saratoga*'s turrets have been located. (Naval History and Heritage Command)

The U.S. Army received *Saratoga*'s 8-inch turrets as well as those of the *Lexington* in February 1942 and quickly mounted them as part of Oahu's defenses. *Saratoga*'s turrets were installed at Brodie Camp on the north shore and at Salt Lake on the south shore. (U.S. Army Museum of Hawaii)

An army corporal poses next to one of the 8-inch guns that were transferred from the *Lexington*-class carriers in early 1942. The army deemed a Japanese invasion of Oahu a very real threat in the early months of the war and took measures to prepare for it. (U.S. Army Museum of Hawaii)

99

Saratoga received more permanent repairs following her first torpedoing and extensive modifications at Naval Yard, Puget Sound, between February and May 1942. As seen in a 14 May 1942 photo, gone were the old foremast and attached compartments, replaced by a smaller mainmast. At the top level of the island to the front of the mainmast is the forward Mk. 37 director, which controlled the new twin 5-inch/38-caliber mounts. The secondary conning station, Pri-Fly, and the catwalks had been removed from the smokestack in mid-1941, when a compartment was mounted on the front of the smokestack to control the CXAM-1 radar at the top front of the smokestack.

In a 14 May 1942 view of the forward part of the *Saratoga* during her refitting at NYPS, the two new forward 5-inch/38-caliber gun mounts are to the right, with the aircraft crane to the front of mount number one. Changes were made to the 5-inch guns in the four sponsons of the carrier; the 12 original 5-inch/25-caliber mounts were replaced by eight single 5-inch/38-caliber mounts, with two per sponson. The sponsons now had splinter shields. At the front end of the forward port sponson at the bottom of the photo is a quad 1.1-inch gun mount. When *Saratoga* completed this refit in late May, she had a complement of nine quad 1.1-inch mounts. This weapon already had proved inadequate.

This overhead view of *Saratoga* dated 14 May 1942 was taken from amidships on the port side looking aft. Life rafts are stowed on the side of the smokestack. During this refit, the top of the smokestack was lowered by one level, somewhat reducing the ship's silhouette. Immediately aft of the smokestack is the newly installed aft Mk. 37 director, topped with the Mk. 4 (FD) fire-control radar antenna. Also to the rear of the smokestack are the two aft twin 5-inch/38-caliber gun mounts, designated, front to rear, mounts three and four. On the near side of the crane boom to the right is a sponson containing 20mm cannon mounts; the cannons themselves, just visible behind their shield, are covered in canvas and elevated near vertical.

Saratoga's amidships area is viewed from the starboard side in a 14 May 1942 photo taken at NYPS. The boxy structure that now occupies the level above the flag bridge in the island is the air-defense bridge, the forward air lookout station, called Sky Forward. This bridge was open, lacking a roof, because it was felt that open bridges were necessary in order to contend with aerial attacks. Although two boats were stowed alongside the island, the boat davits abeam the base of the smokestack had been replaced by six individual platforms for 20mm cannons. On the second level between the island and the smokestack was a platform and splinter shield for a quad 1.1-inch gun mount.

Saratoga's new forward twin 5-inch/38-caliber gun mounts and her redesigned island are viewed from the flight deck. A tilted railing was installed around the platform for the superfiring, or upper, 5-inch mount. The ship's bell still hangs from the front of the navigating bridge. Above the air-defense bridge is the Mk. 4 (FD) radar antenna on the Mk. 37 director. The CXAM-1 radar antenna is visible atop the front of the smokestack.

The port sides of the second-from-forward twin 5-inch/38-caliber gun mount and the island are viewed on 14 May 1942. Unlike the former 8-inch turrets, which were numbered one to four, forward to aft, the 5-inch gun mounts were counted consecutively, whether they were single mounts in sponsons or twin mounts with gun houses. Thus, the twin 5-inch mounts were numbered, fore to aft, mounts number five, six, seven, and eight.

"SC-1" ANTENNA

"CXAM-1" ANTENNA

"SG" ANTENNA

"FD" ANTENNA

NOTE: REFLECTOR
EXTENSION WILL INTERFERE
WITH PARTLY OPEN HATCH—
WHEN ANTENNA IS
DEPRESSED AND
CROSS-LEVELED

Mounted in the new air-defense bridge, seen from overhead on 14 May 1942, is the Mk. 37 director. Within partitions on the sides of this bridge are seats for aircraft spotters, equipped with binocular rests. Also documented in the photo are the recently installed SG surface-search radar antenna on the main mast at the level of the yardarm, the CXAM-1 "mattress" radar antenna at the top front of the smokestack, and the SC-1 radar antenna, at the top rear of the smokestack, mostly used for air search.

The forward Mk. 37 director and the Mk. 4 (FD) fire-control radar antenna on *Saratoga* are viewed from the front on 14 May 1942. Three ports with hinged covers were provided for the operators' telescopes; above those covers were spotting hatches. The operators tracked enemy aircraft with the director, which sent data to a fire-control computer, which generated firing solutions for the 5-inch guns. Thus, the gun mounts could be automatically controlled or, if necessary, manually controlled by their crews.

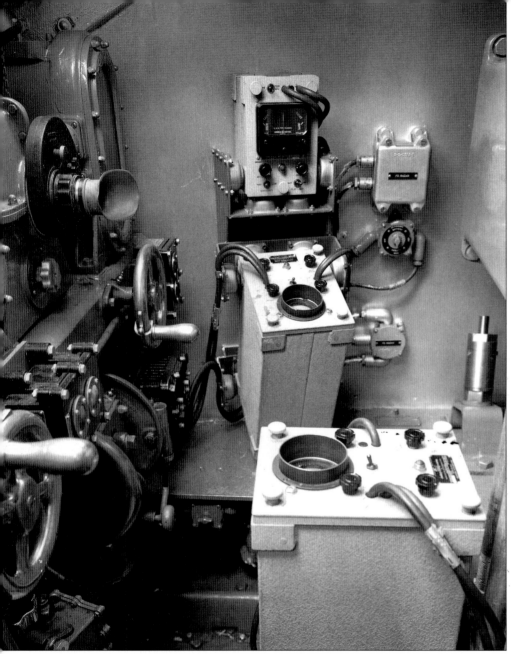

Within the turret-like body of the Mk. 37 director, the pointer's and trainer's stations are viewed from the control officer's station on the left side of the compartment. The control officer had command of the director and designated targets using a slewing scope. The pointer kept the horizontal crosshair of the director's sight on the target, while the trainer kept the vertical crosshair on target. Also stationed inside the director were several talkers, a radar operator, and an operator for the director's optical rangefinder.

A 14 May 1942 photograph shows In the foreground the installation on the foremast of the SG radar waveguide, a hollow metal conductor that guided radar microwaves. In the background is the front of the smokestack, searchlight platforms protruding from each side; a 36-inch searchlight is on the port platform. At the same level as the searchlight platforms is the CXAM-1 radar control booth, installed in 1941 at the former location of Pri-Fly and the secondary conning tower. Above the booth is the CXAM-1 platform.

A wartime color photograph of the *Saratoga* shows her configuration from the time she left the Navy Yard, Puget Sound, with her new twin 5-inch/38-caliber gun mounts on 14 May 1942 until she was fitted with extensive galleries along the flight deck for a 20mm gun gallery during a refit at Pearl Harbor following her torpedoing on 31 August 1942. During that interim, *Saratoga* was painted in Measure 11; although originally specified as a scheme of overall Sea Blue (5-S), by early 1942 the Navy had in practice revised Measure 11 to overall Navy Blue (5-N). The aircraft parked on deck are Wildcat fighters, Dauntless dive bombers, and Avenger torpedo bombers. (Naval History and Heritage Command)

Mk 37 Gun Director

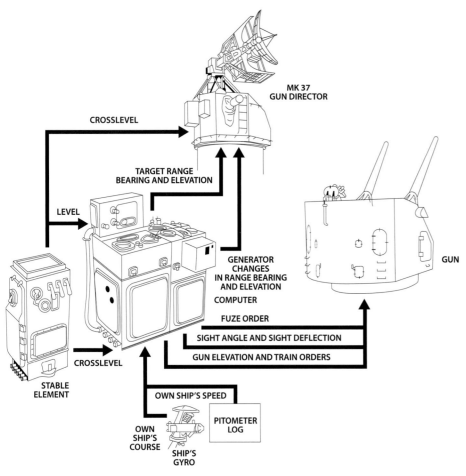

The Mk. 37 secondary battery director usually was tasked with tracking enemy aircraft and ships, primarily destroyers, and establishing their range, bearing, and, in the case of aircraft, altitude. Those data were transmitted to the plotting room ("Plot"), where analog computers, working with stable elements, which corrected for the pitch and roll of the ship, and the ship's gyro and pitometer, which provided information on the ship's course and speed, calculated within seconds the firing solution for the 5-inch guns. Plot sent that data to the director as well as the 5-inch turret and also controlled the train (traverse) and elevation of both the guns and the director. However, the director also made corrections to the target bearing, range, and angle of attack. Also, although the directors normally controlled the aiming and firing of the 5-inch guns, Plot or the gun crews could control the guns when necessary. Plot would control the guns when firing at targets ashore.

108

Fully repaired and refitted, USS *Saratoga* is anchored at Pearl Harbor on 6 June 1942. *Saratoga* had missed the Battle of Midway, but in this photo her flight deck is stocked with new Grumman Avenger torpedo bombers, which the carrier would ferry to Midway.

USS *Saratoga*, in the foreground, and USS *Enterprise* (CV-6) were photographed together in the Solomon Islands in August 1942. Both of these carriers, along with USS *Wasp* (CV-7) formed the cores of separate task forces in the Guadalcanal Campaign. (National Museum of Naval Aviation)

After seeing combat in the Battle of the Eastern Solomons on 24 August 1942, USS *Saratoga* was steaming south away from the Solomons at 0747 on the morning of 31 August when I-26, a Japanese B1-type submarine shown in this photograph, launched several torpedoes at her. Of three torpedoes spotted running toward the carrier, one detonated on her starboard side at frame 133, causing flooding in boiler rooms 13 and 15. Within 45 minutes, the carrier had developed a six-degree list to starboard, but two hours later the list was corrected. The ship's electrical system, necessary for propulsion, was damaged but through heroic efforts was repaired. On 6 September the *Saratoga* reached the safety of Tongatabu Island. Submarine I-26 went on to further exploits, including putting a fatal torpedo into the cruiser USS *Juneau* (CL-52) off Guadalcanal on 13 November 1942. Following the Battle off Samar, I-26 was sunk on or around 25 October 1944.

Saratoga's engineers induced a list of 9.5 degrees to port when she was photographed at Tongatabu on 9 September 1942, three days after her arrival at that island. There, the ship underwent temporary repairs until 12 September, when she departed for Pearl Harbor.

On 3 September 1942, three days after her torpedoing by I-26, *Saratoga* steams under her own power toward Tongatabu. Although most of the carrier's air group had flown off the ship for Espiritu Santo shortly after the torpedoing, a few planes are still visible on deck.

At Tongatabu on 10 September 1942, part of the starboard stability blister has been removed around where the torpedo struck. Visible inside the opening is the armor belt that protected the vital internal machinery spaces of the hull from torpedo and shell hits.

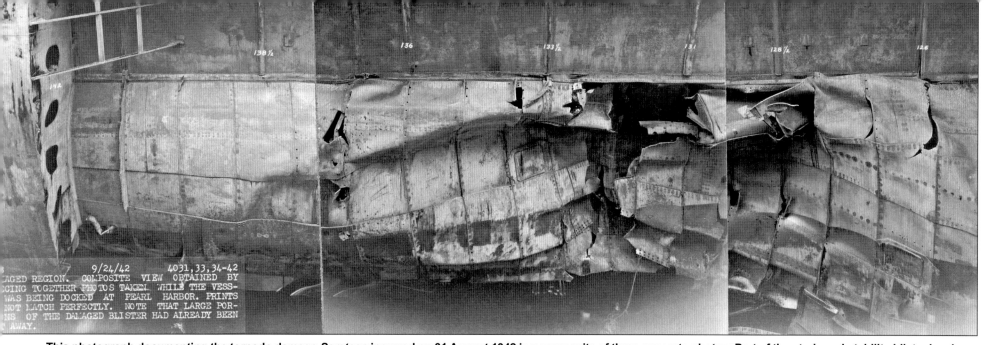

This photograph documenting the torpedo damage *Saratoga* incurred on 31 August 1942 is a composite of three separate photos. Part of the starboard stability blister has been cut away, exposing the area around frame 133 where the torpedo breached the hull.

A photograph taken while USS *Saratoga* was dry-docked at Pearl Harbor on 24 September 1942 looks downward at the torpedo-damaged area. Repairs on the ship would continue through October and early November, with other modifications being perfomed.

Being built at Pearl Harbor on 3 October 1942 is a large replacement section to be installed in the torpedo-damaged area on the starboard side of *Saratoga's* hull. It was necessary to rebuild the network of damaged tanks inboard of the stability blister.

Repairs on her hull and other modifications completed, *Saratoga* stood out from Pearl Harbor on 6 November 1942. Prominent in this aerial view dated five days later are new sponsons alongside and just below the flight deck for a battery of 20mm guns.

A 20 November 1942 overhead photo of *Saratoga* shows her in her configuration following the September-November 1942 repairs and modifications. On her flight deck is a mix of aircraft, including Grumman TBFs and F4Fs, Douglas SDBs, and Vought F4Us.

A view off *Saratoga's* starboard bow shows the carrier on 6 November 1942, the date the carrier left Pearl Harbor following her September-November repairs and modifications. Among other changes, nine quad 40mm mounts had replaced the 1.1-inch gun mounts.

Saratoga is viewed from off her port stern on 6 November 1942. During the refitting that had just concluded, four 20mm gun mounts were installed in the two gun tubs below the ramp of the flight deck. By this point, *Saratoga* had 52 20mm gun mounts on board.

In another photo taken at Pearl Harbor on 6 November 1942, *Saratoga* is viewed from directly abaft. The two gun tubs below the ramp of the flight deck are visible; each one contained two 20mm gun mounts with armored shields. Above and to the left of the gun tub to the port side of the ramp is the landing signal officer's (LSO) platform. This officer stationed himself on the platform during aircraft landing operations, using hand-held paddles to signal if the aircraft was too low or too high to make a safe landing. *Saratoga* was now painted in Measure 21, overall Navy Blue.

In the spring and summer of 1943, HMS *Victorious* (right) joined USS *Saratoga* (left) as part of Task Force 14, spending much of that time engaged in training exercises off New Caledonia. They were photographed together at Noumea, New Caledonia, in that period. (US Naval Institute)

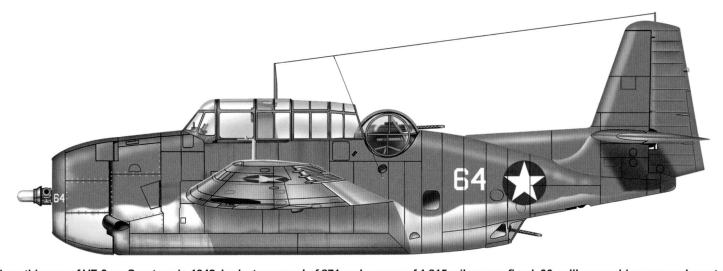

The Grumman TBF-1, such as this one of VF-8 on *Saratoga* in 1942, had a top speed of 271 mph; range of 1,215 miles; one fixed .30-caliber machine gun and one turret-mounted .50-caliber machine gun; and carried a torpedo or 2,000 pounds of bombs or depth charges.

Saratoga had a well-equipped sheet-metal shop, where a variety of repairs and fabrication were carried out. The man to the left is operating a brake, a large tool for bending sheet metal along a straight line. The men to the right are working on a rack. (National Archives via Rob Stern)

The crew of any naval ship might spend day after day on alert or in active operations, getting scant sleep. Thus, they would grab any opportunity to sleep or relax, such as these two *Saratoga* crewmen suspended over the sea on one of the life nets that surrounded the carrier's flight deck.

On 5 and 11 November 1943, *Saratoga*'s Air Group 12 raided the Japanese naval base at Simpson Harbor, Rabaul, temporarily incapacitating Admiral Takeo Kurita's Second Fleet. Here, Grumman F6F Hellcats are being recovered following a Rabaul raid. (Stan Piet collection)

Hellcats are being recovered on *Saratoga*. In the foreground, an airdale stands by as a Hellcat on the forward elevator is being lowered to the hangar deck. *Saratoga*'s Air Group 12 began receiving Grumman F6F Hellcats in October and November 1943.

An F6F approaching the forward elevator on *Saratoga* in November 1943 is poised on the flap doors that were designed to be opened to accommodate extra-long aircraft on the elevator. The plane parker in the white helmet is signaling the pilot into position.

Prior to takeoff on a November 1943 raid on Rabaul, left to right, Ens. Charles W. Miller, Lt. (j.g.) Henry H. Dearing, and Lt. (j.g.) "Bus" Alber of VF-12 proceed to their F6F Hellcats. Miller's gloves are clutched in his teeth, and the pilots are carrying chart boards.

The launch officer on the *Saratoga* is about to swing his flag down, signaling Commander Joseph "Jumping Joe" Clifton of VF-12 to take off the *Saratoga* in 1943. The plane's nickname, *Sally Darlin*, is painted on the side of the cowl.

Another F6F prepares to take off from *Saratoga* as the launch officer waves his flag, signaling the pilot to rev his engine, and airdales watch expectantly. In the background is the smokestack, with life rafts and emergency bags of provisions stowed on its side.

During a lull in the action, crewmen of the *Saratoga* congregate around the two forward 5-inch/38-caliber gun mounts, talking shop or shooting the breeze. Lying flush on the flight deck to the left and oriented forward to aft is the lowered palisade

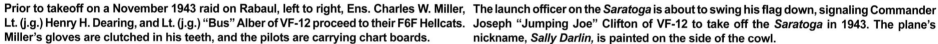

USS *Saratoga* Late 1943

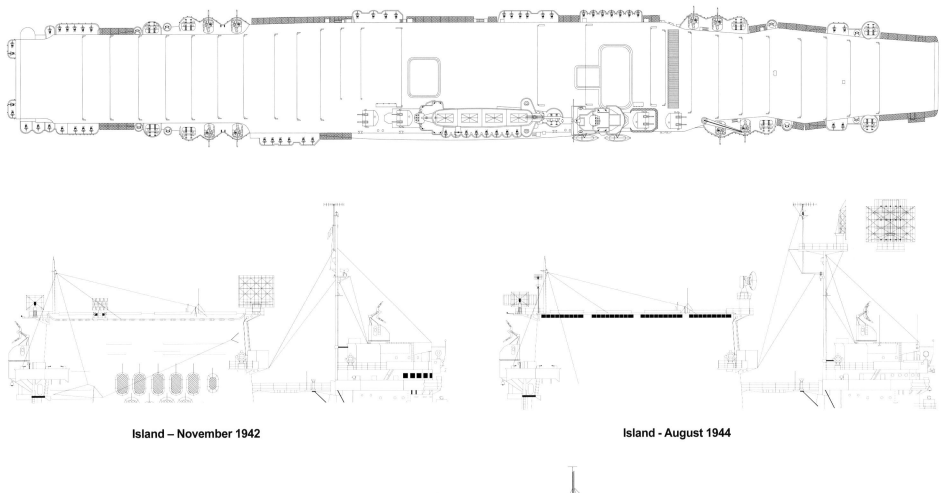

Island – November 1942

Island - August 1944

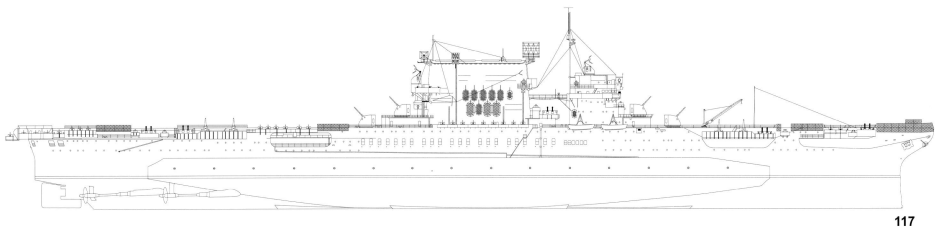

Officers and crewmen are spectators as an aircraft comes in for a landing on the *Saratoga*. Hopefully the plane's tail hook will catch an arrestor wire; if not, the barrier wires are designed to keep the plane from crashing into the aircraft in the foreground.

Saratoga personnel gather around an SBD dive bomber and on platforms and catwalks of the island and smokestack as an F6F approaches after a raid on Rabaul, in November 1943. Aircraft recovery operations often attracted the keen interest of crewmen.

A Douglas SBD-5 Dauntless of VB-12 is depicted at the time of the 1943 Rabaul raids. The SBD-4 had a maximum speed of 255 miles per hour, range of 1,115 miles, and was armed with two fixed and two flex-mounted .50-caliber machine guns and 2,250 pounds of bombs.

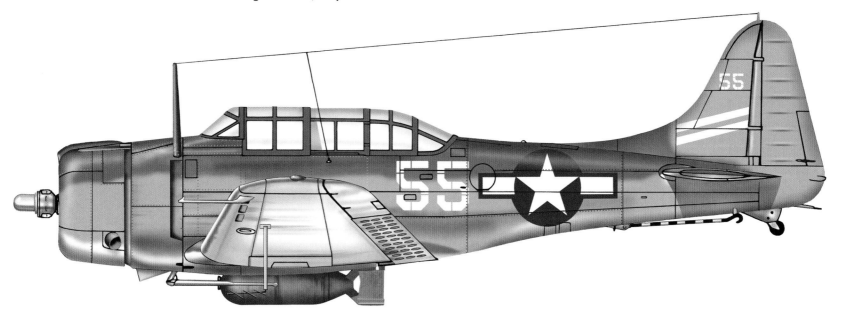

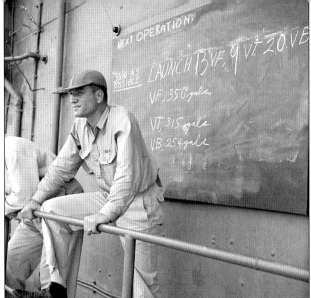

Lt. Wayne Miller, who photographed scenes aboard USS *Saratoga* in the latter part of 1943, took this study of crewmen on the flight deck of the carrier. To the upper left is what appears to be the forward left part of a 5-inch gun house; a bomb is to the bottom.

On a catwalk on the aerologic level of the island of the *Saratoga*, Commander Roland Stieler observes the launching of aircraft bound for a raid on Rabaul in November 1943. The blackboard behind him contained information on the next flight operation.

In what could pass for a portrait of a crusty old fisherman in a storm, Capt. John Howard Cassidy, commander of the *Saratoga*, stares intently into the distance in a 1943 photo by Lt. Wayne Miller. Cassidy commanded the ship from 23 August 1943 to 22 June 1944.

Spectators view flight operations on *Saratoga* during the fall of 1943. The upper level in the photo is the port side of the flag bridge. The next level below is the navigating bridge. To the bottom left is the signal board with stop, caution, and go lights, seen earlier.

In another photograph by Wayne Miller from the fall of 1943, crewmen on the USS *Saratoga* take a break. One sailor entertains his shipmates with an accordion while others sunbathe. The old salt in the left background displays numerous tattoos.

On the *Saratoga* on 5 November 1943, mess attendants listen raptly to news of the successful raid on Rabaul. During World War II, the U.S. Navy remained a segregated institution, and African Americans and Filipinos served primarily as mess attendants.

119

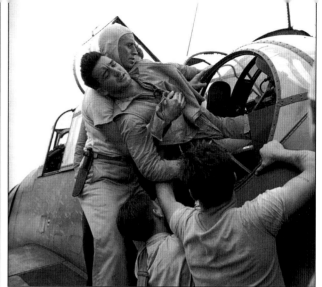

One of *Saratoga*'s corpsmen, John W. Galbreath, of Sebastopol, California, stands ready to help the wounded when planes return from the 5 November 1943 Rabaul raid. Corpsmen were the Navy's enlisted medical specialists: true heroes in their own right. Aircraft returning from the raid would bring injured men requiring corpsmen's help.

Emergency crewmen rush to extricate wounded crewmen from an Avenger torpedo bomber on *Saratoga* after the 5 November 1943 attack on Rabaul. The pilot, Air Group 12 Commander Henry H. Caldwell exits the aircraft in the background. On the opposite side of the plane a rescue scenario was unfolding, documented in the next photo.

In one of the iconic images of World War II, shot by Wayne Miller, emergency crewmen extricate gunner Kenneth Bratton, a member of Cdr. Caldwell's crew who suffered a shattered knee, from the side hatch of the turret of an Avenger. Bratton applied a tourniquet to his knee after it was wounded, and he survived the severe injury.

While his concerned pilot looks on, Aviation Radioman Petty Officer 1st Class (ARM1) Alva Parker of VB-12 is helped out of the cockpit of an SBD aboard the *Saratoga* after the 5 November 1943 raid on Rabaul. Parker, who operated the radio and the flexible machine guns, had suffered shrapnel wounds in the shoulders and neck.

A VT-12 aircrewman with neck and head wounds lies in a stretcher on the USS *Saratoga* following a November 1943 raid on Rabaul, waiting to be transported below decks to an aid station. Marked on his inflatable life vest above his left hand is "Riser, G. E. / VT-12." It is not clear if Riser was his full surname or the last part of his surname.

In November 1943, three officers discuss matters in the chart house, located on the navigating-bridge level aft of the pilot house. To the right is the ship's navigator. They are leaning on a plotting board marking all identified forces, enemy and friendly. (National Archives via Rob Stern)

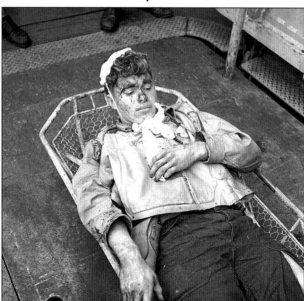

Lieutenant Commander Vincent L. Hathorn, commander of VB-12 on USS *Saratoga*, confers with Cdr. Joseph C. "Jumping Joe" Clifton, commander of Carrier Air Group 12, following a raid on an enemy base. Hathorn, on the left wears a flight helmet, goggles, and parachute harness and is holding a plotting board. Clifton wears a zippered flight suit.

Aircrewmen on USS *Saratoga* partake of sandwiches and fruit after a mission in late 1943. On the *Saratoga*, as on other U.S. Navy ships, there were crew messes that operated around the clock, and officers' wardrooms served food at set times, but in times of combat or alerts, cold sandwiches were made available to the ships' crews.

Happy crewmen gather around the pilots in the foreground from *Saratoga*'s Air Group 12, just back from a raid on Rabaul in November 1943. The pilots are recounting some aspect of the mission to the lieutenant in the fore-and-aft cap. A successful raid or mission was cause for jubilation and encouragement on an aircraft carrier.

Air Group 12 Commander Henry H. Caldwell, right, briefs news correspondents before a November 1943 attack on Rabaul. News reports of the Navy's successful operations were instrumental in sustaining morale on the home front, but reporting was subject to some censorship and controls, and news media sometimes exercised self-censorship.

Avenger torpedo-bomber crewmen of VT-12 wind down and compare notes after their return to *Saratoga* from a raid on Rabaul. They were identified as (left to right): Aviation Machinist's Mate R. E. Blakemaoorm [sic], Aviation Radioman Johnny Taylor, Aviation Radioman Blackie Sherrod, and Aviation Ordnanceman Joe Reininger.

Officers pass the time in one of *Saratoga*'s wardrooms. Here, officers were served their meals and relaxed when off duty. A backgammon game is going on in the foreground while others read or play cards. The photographer of this image and many others shown here, Wayne Miller, was a member of Edward Steichen's Naval Aviation Photographic Unit.

Messmen relax on the *Saratoga*. In the 1930s and World War II, African Americans who enlisted in the U.S. Navy were restricted to the Messman Branch, comprising stewards, mess attendants, officers' cooks, and commissarymen. Filipinos, Guamanians, and persons of Chinese ancestry also filled the ranks of the Messman Branch in this period.

An intelligence officer debriefs pilots on USS *Saratoga* after a mission in the fall of 1943. Debriefing, or interrogating pilots about the mission, was necessary for assessing the effectiveness of planning for the mission, estimating the level of damage inflicted on the enemy, and gaining intelligence on enemy positions, forces, and movements.

The interior of *Saratoga*'s pilot house is viewed from the forward port corner facing to the starboard side of the compartment. The helmsman in the foreground steers the ship with the lever instead of a wheel. To his front are two compass repeaters. (National Archives via Rob Stern)

Photographer Wayne Miller took this portrait of Admiral Arthur W. Radford on the *Saratoga* in the fall of 1943. Admiral Radford (1896-1973) was instrumental in the creation of the Naval Aviation Photographic Unit. As commander of Carrier Division 1 in 1943, he had *Saratoga* as his flagship. Later, he served as commander-in-chief, U.S. Pacific Command (CINCPAC) and, from 1953 to 1957, as chairman of the Joint Chiefs of Staff.

A crewman takes a break on the roof of one of *Saratoga*'s twin 5-inch/38-caliber gun mounts. The guns are pointed skyward, at the ready should they need to leap into action against enemy aircraft. Projecting from the side of the gun house of the mount are protective hoods for the pointer's and the sight-checker's telescopes.

Crewmen operate controls and closely monitor the gauges on one of the *Saratoga*'s boilers. The man at the center wears protective gloves, and to the right is a talker. *Saratoga*'s 16 boilers produced steam to generate electrical power via four GE turbo generators to drive the ship's eight 22,500-shaft-horsepower electric motors, which in turn powered the four propellers.

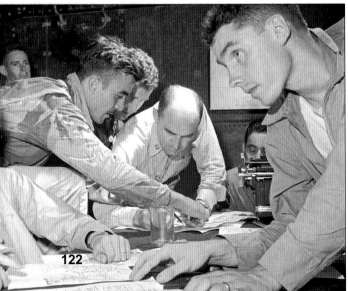

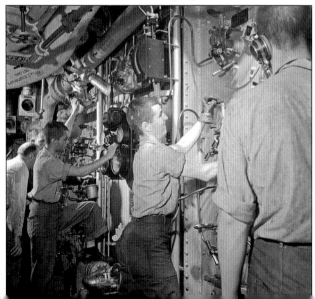

Saratoga operated in the vicinity of Noumea for 12 months, beginning in December 1942, providing air cover for U.S. forces in the Eastern Solomon Islands. Between 17 May and 31 July 1943, she was aided by the British carrier, HMS *Victorious;* and, on 20 October, she was at last joined by a second U.S. carrier, the *Princeton* (CVL-23), the duo forming the nucleus of Task Force 38.

During the assault on Bougainville on 1 November 1943, *Saratoga's* aircraft, along with those of the *Princeton,* struck Japanese airfields on nearby Buka. Reacting to reports of Japanese cruisers concentrating at Rabaul, on 5 November 1943 *Saratoga's* Air Group 12 attacked the Japanese fleet, conducting what was in essence a successful assault on a Japanese Pearl Harbor, disabling most of the Japanese cruisers. Upon *Saratoga's* return to Espiritu Santo on 5 November, Admiral Halsey declared that the raid had saved the lives of thousands of Marines at Bougainville.

Not resting on their laurels, *Saratoga* and *Princeton* raided Rabaul again on 11 November.

The two carriers were designated the Relief Carrier Group for the Gilberts campaign and, after striking Nauru on 19 November, rendezvoused on 23 November with Task Groups 54.8 and 54.9, plus Task Unit 16.10.2. On 27 November, *Saratoga, Princeton, North Carolina,* Battleship Division 6, and eight destroyers were designated Task Group 50.2, with Rear Admiral Arthur D. Radford as commander. On 30 November the F6F Hellcats of *Saratoga's* VF-12 flew to Tarawa, where they would operate from newly captured airfields. The same day, *Saratoga,* having steamed over a year without repairs, at last turned her bow toward Pearl Harbor, and then on to the United States.

This view from the air-defense bridge reveals the color and markings of the forward flight deck. A whip antenna is in the foreground. Below is the top of the aircraft crane to the front of the superstructure.

Commander Dayton Brown took this photo of USS *Saratoga* from a boat speeding away from the carrier, giving a unique view of the port side of the ship at anchor in South Pacific coastal waters. A close examination of the photo reveals that a torpedo net has been installed around the ship. Present along the flight deck amidships are 20mm mounts that would be removed in a refitting in December 1943, when new quad 40mm mounts and sponsons would also be fitted. Thus, the photo predates that refitting.

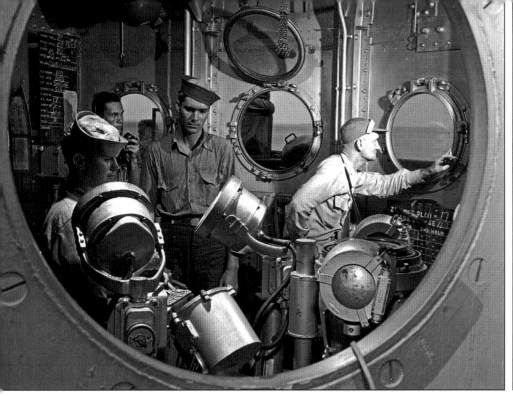

Photographer Wayne Miller took this view through a porthole into the pilot house of Saratoga in late 1943. This was where the ship was navigated during normal conditions. Seated in the captain's chair is an officer who appears to be Capt. John Cassidy.

Tending to the spiritual needs of members of the USS Saratoga's crew, the chaplain, Commander Elbert C. Cole Jr., holds religious services aboard the carrier in the fall of 1943. The location seems to be a pilots' ready room equipped with stationary seats.

This undated view of USS Saratoga probably was taken in the second half of 1943. The aircraft on the flight deck have the national insignia with bars, which was introduced in mid-1943, but the 40mm mounts of the December 1943 refit are not yet present.

During a December 1943 refitting at Hunter's Point Naval Shipyard, the *Saratoga*'s complement of 40mm gun mounts was greatly increased while her 20mm gun mounts were correspondingly decreased. This view documents some of the new mounts.

A photo dated 2 January 1944 at Hunter's Point indicates new quad 40mm gun mounts on the port side of the ship from amidships forward. Also indicated are smaller tubs containing Mk. 51 directors, which automatically controlled the 40mm mounts.

A distant view of the port side of USS *Saratoga* on 2 January 1944 indicates all of the new quad 40mm gun mounts and directors recently installed. This refitting brought the *Saratoga*'s total complement of 40mm mounts to 23 quad and two twin mounts.

USS *Saratoga* Sectional View

When *Saratoga* was anchored in a secure area, the crew was often given the opportunity to swim. Such is the case in this photo taken at Kwajalein in February 1944. Some men are using the top of the starboard stability blister as a convenient diving platform.

Located in the depths of the hull of *Saratoga* was the IC compartment, which contained the ship's master gyroscope, the large, drum-shaped structure in the foreground, and the ship's main telephone switchboard. (National Archives via Rob Stern)

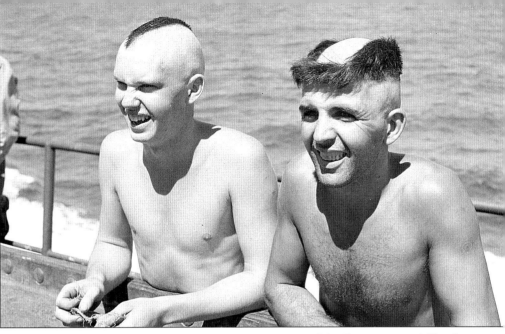

USS *Saratoga* had a fully equipped dental office, located on the second deck in the bow of the ship. When the weather was warm, it got hot below decks, and the spotlights added to the ambient heat, so here the dental staff are dressed in t-shirts to keep cool. (National Archives via Rob Stern)

The shellbacks of USS *Saratoga* threw another crossing-of-the-line party on 6 March 1944 when the carrier once again crossed the equator. Two of the ship's crewmen have had their hair cut in unusual ways as part of their initiation from polliwogs to shellbacks – seamen who have crossed the equator.

For several days beginning 12 March 1944, *Saratoga* was battered by heavy seas occasioned by a storm while steaming from Espiritu Santo to Hobart, Tasmania. In this photo, waves crash over the bow of the carrier.

In the March 1944 storm, crashing waves and buffeting to the carrier caused considerable damage, mostly to the exterior of the ship, but also to some interior spaces and machinery. As seen here, the damages including buckling of the bow ramp.

As indicated here, the storm sheared off the number-one Mk. 51 director and tub at frame 3. Also carried away was the number-two Mk. 51 director and tub at frame 3 on the port side of the ship. Life nets, antennas, and fuel lines were also swept away.

Below the folded wing of the forwardmost Grumman F6F Hellcat is the location where the March 1944 storm carried away Mk. 51 director number two and its tub. The sponson of quad 40mm gun mount number two, below the wing of the second F6F, was damaged.

A photograph dated 20 March 1944 documents a tear in the underside of the sponson of the number-two 40mm gun mount of USS *Saratoga* caused by the storm. The quad 40mm gun barrels protrude from the sponson. A section of life net remains intact.

A close-up of the port bow of *Saratoga* shows the area where the number-two Mk. 51 director and its tub were sheared away from the shell of the hull during the March 1944 storm. Life nets were also sheared off. Waving above the flight deck is the jack.

An 11 April 1944 photograph shows a section of new catwalk and safety railing along and just below the edge of the forward starboard side of the flight deck. This replaced the old life nets along the flight deck. In the foreground is an aircraft refueling station.

From March to May 1944 the *Saratoga* was attached to the British Eastern Fleet, commanded by Vice Adm. Sir A. J. Powers. While operating with the fleet in the Indian Ocean in April, Capt. John Cassidy, left, met with Adm. Lord Louis Mountbatten.

On the flight deck of *Saratoga*, anchored at Tricomalee, Ceylon (now Sri Lanka) on 30 April 1944, Adm. Lord Louis Mountbatten, supreme commander of the Southeast Asia Area, addresses personnel of the carrier. He is to the right of center in a white uniform.

During *Saratoga*'s 1944 cruise with the Eastern Fleet, Vice Adm. Clement Moody, commander of carriers, Royal Navy, visited the ship. Moody is at the center of the photo, having just flown in on a Barracuda torpedo bomber, and is being rendered honors.

One of the sailors' favorite attractions on the *Saratoga* was the gedunk, as the soda fountain was nicknamed. The ship originally did not have a gedunk, but one was installed in her before the war, and she kept the crew supplied with sodas, ice cream, and snacks. (National Archives via Rob Stern)

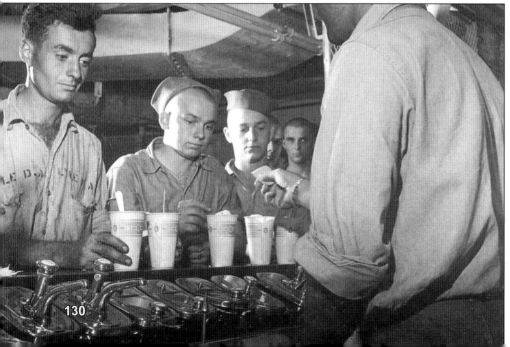

Supplies are being transferred either from or to a landing craft alongside *Saratoga* at Trincomalee, Ceylon, on 16 May 1944. This photo gives a good sense of the width of the of the starboard stability blister. From its launching, *Saratoga* had experienced a tendency to a starboard list because of the large mass of the island and smokestack on the starboard side of the ship. Plans were formulated by the late 1930s to install a blister extending above and below the waterline on the starboard side of the hull to improve the ship's stability. However, this blister was not added until 1941. A narrower blister was also added to the port side of the hull. (National Archives via Rob Stern)

This photo and the following series document some of the major changes made to USS *Saratoga* during her 1944 refitting at the Navy Yard, Puget Sound, in Bremerton, Washington. The carrier's Measure 21 scheme had been painted-over in Measure 32/11-A, a disruptive scheme containing Light Gray (5-L), Ocean Gray (5-O), and Dull Black (BK), and meant to disguise the bearing and identity of the ship. The SK radar antenna had been removed from the top front of the smokestack, and the new SM radar antenna was mounted in its place. (US Naval Institute)

Among changes to the starboard bow, the Mk. 51 director and tub swept away in the March 1944 storm have been replaced. The cover over the hawse pipe for the starboard anchor dated to the fall of 1942, when the starboard anchor and chain had been deleted. (The Floating Drydock)

The sponson on the starboard side just forward of the forward twin 5-inch/38-caliber gun mount is shown in a photo dated 13 August 1944. Many of the gun sponsons that had been damaged in the March 1944 storm were repaired during this refitting at NYPS. (The Floating Drydock)

The two forward twin 5-inch gun mounts and the forward part of the island are viewed. The boom of the aircraft crane is lowered to the deck. The capacity of this crane had just been increased from 10,000 pounds to 20,000 pounds by modification of the crane boom. (The Floating Drydock)

The foremast and island of *Saratoga* are in view. A Mk. 22 "orange peel" antenna had been added to the right side of the FD radar antenna on each Mk. 37 director. The SK radar antenna, formerly on the top of the smokestack, was now on the foremast. (The Floating Drydock)

The port side of the smokestack is viewed at NYPS in August 1944. The three sponsons along the base of the smokestack were installed during a refitting in December 1943 at Hunter's Point. Two tubs with Mk. 51 directors are the next level up on the smokestack.

Mounted on brackets projecting aft of the top rear of the smokestack is the SC-3 radar antenna, which had replaced the SC-1 radar antenna during the December 1943 refitting. Below the SC-3 is the aft Mk. 37 director with the FD and Mk. 22 radar antennas on top.

The island and adjacent structures are viewed from the starboard side in a photo dated 13 August 1944. The SM radar antenna is visible at the top front of the smokestack. This dish antenna was six feet in diameter and was linked to a height-finder radar set used for controlling the carrier's fighter aircraft. On the side of the hull, the ventilator doors, present on the ship from its beginning, are open. Two motor whaleboats are stowed on the side of the ship. (The Floating Drydock)

In the December 1943 refitting, all of the boat bays or boat pockets had been fitted with sponsons and quad 40mm gun mounts. These replaced 20mm gun mounts installed earlier in the war. The two mounts in the port boat bay are visible in this August 1944 photo. (The Floating Drydock)

The aft starboard quarter of *Saratoga* is viewed at the Navy Yard, Puget Sound, in August 1944. From right to left are two single 5-inch/38-caliber mounts, a quad 40mm mount, a Mk. 51 director, a quad 40mm mount, Mk. 51 director, and six 20mm mounts. (National Archives)

The flight deck and part of the smokestack of *Saratoga* are viewed from the port side of the ship at NYPS in August 1944. Parked alongside the smokestack is a portable crane. Below the edge of the flight deck are some of the recently installed catwalks and railings. (National Archives)

The port side of the smokestack is seen in this photo dated 13 August 1944. A significant detail is the fact that the insides of the doors of the deck house adjoining the rear of the smokestack are painted in the same camouflage patterns as the exterior of the doors. (The Floating Drydock)

Essentially the same scene portrayed in the preceding photo is viewed from a slightly different angle. A clear view is offered of the aft Mk. 37 director and its foundation resting on the bipod mainmast. The small structure between the lower parts of the legs of the mainmast housed a boatswain's and deck-gear locker as well as the Radar IV compartment. The deck house below twin 5-inch/38-caliber gun mount number seven (the next-to-rear twin 5-inch mount) contained that mount's ready-service ammunition storage and handling room, a 40mm ready-service ammunition compartment, and a crew's shelter. (The Floating Drydock)

Saratoga's smokestack and island are observed from the aft port quarter in another photo taken at the Navy Yard, Puget Sound, on 13 August 1944. The newly installed SM radar antenna dominates the top front of the smokestack. Below that radar installation on the front of the smokestack is a searchlight platform. On each wing of the platform is a 36-inch searchlight. Leading aft from the platform is a catwalk, ending with a vertical ladder up to an access door high up on the smokestack. Also below the searchlight platform is a catwalk and safety rails leading forward to the aft end of the navigating bridge level. Below that catwalk is a quad 40mm gun mount. (The Floating Drydock)

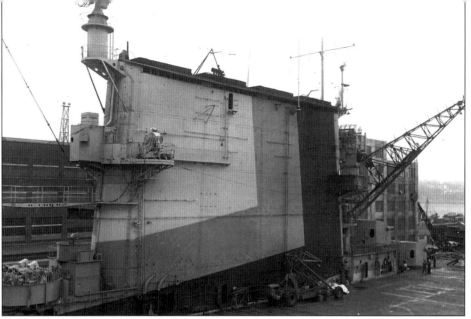

The port side of the smokestack appears in a 13 August 1944 photo. The compartment at the front of the smokestack on the same level as the 36-inch searchlight platform housed Radar II. To the bottom left, aft of the 40mm gun mount is its Mk. 51 director. (The Floating Drydock)

A photo dated 6 September 1944 taken from a dock at the Navy Yard, Puget Sound, shows the port side of the smokestack after the summer 1944 refitting. The SM radar antenna is at the front of the stack and the SC-3 radar antenna is at the rear of the stack. (National Archives, San Bruno, via Tracy White)

A longstanding weakness of USS *Saratoga* was the slowness of her forward elevator. This situation caused lengthy turnaround times in moving aircraft down to the hangar deck or bringing aircraft up to the flight deck, and such delays could prove disastrous in battle. Thus, during the summer 1944 refitting, the existing elevator machinery was removed, including piping, electrical gear, guides and guide racks, and new, faster-acting equipment was installed except for the stanchion motors and controllers, which were not to be installed until the elevator was enlarged. A long-anticipated enlarged forward elevator was not installed until 1945. (The Floating Drydock)

USS *Saratoga* 1944 Measure 32/11-A

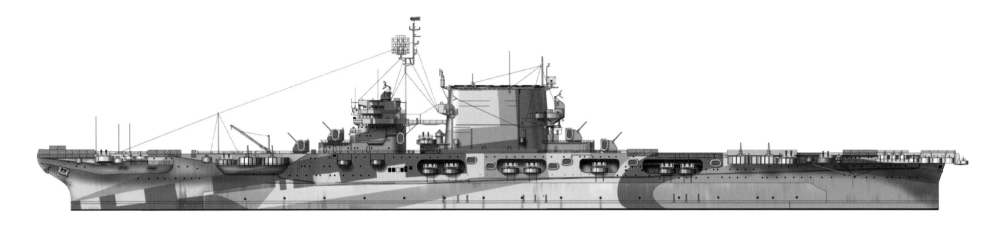

Camouflage Measure 32 was created in 52 different designs ranging from 11A to 35D. The objective of this Measure was three-fold – foremost to deceive enemy observers with regard to the course of the ship; secondly to prevent determination of the type of vessel, and finally to provide some degree of concealment. The Bureau of Ships prepared drawings of these schemes, which were to be used by the yards when applying the paint. *Saratoga,* as well as certain Escort and Light Carriers wore the Measure 32 variation designated Design 11A. There were six variations of Design 11: 11A, 11D, 11F, 11L, 11P, and 11T. The suffix letter was indicative as to the type of ship for which it was created. Design 11A was for aircraft carriers, 11D was for destroyers, 11F was for cargo ships, 11L for amphibious ships and crafts, and 11P for patrol vessels. Suffix codes for other ship types, while not included in Design 11, were B for battleships, C for cruisers, M for mine vessels, SS for submarines and T for transports.

The disruptive pattern of Measure 32/11A was asymmetrical, with the port and starboard schemes being different. The regulations concerning the application of this scheme stated that the pattern need not be exact, or carried into corners, and that small gear, wires, and rigging, as well as areas permanently in shadow, such as those under boats, need not be repainted with the scheme. *Saratoga,* being painted in the shipyard rather than by the ship's own force, wore a more precisely applied and defined scheme than many other vessels.

Saratoga would not see combat while wearing this scheme. Despite the obvious considerable effort and expense applying the scheme during her June through August 1944 overhaul at Bremerton, a collision with a destroyer off Hawaii in November that year forced her to undergo repair work in Pearl Harbor, where, in conjunction with the repairs, *Saratoga* was also repainted in overall blue per Measure 21.

On 7 September 1944 the starboard side of *Saratoga* was photographed at the Navy Yard, Puget Sound, at Bremerton, Washington. The geometric designs of the camouflage were intended to confuse enemy spotters at close range as to the carrier's identity and bearing.

The patterns of the Measure 32/11-A disruptive camouflage on the port side of *Saratoga* were quite different from those on her starboard side, as demonstrated in this 7 September 1944 photo. A large portion of the ship's company is present on deck.

On 8 September 1944, *Saratoga* is conducting post-refitting trials on Puget Sound. During this refitting the flight deck had been sprayed with a stain tinted to the color Formula 21, which most likely was a close match to Deck Blue (20-B).

Faintly visible on the forward and aft ends of the flight deck of *Saratoga* in another photo dated 8 September 1944 is the number 3. This was in a slightly darker color than the flight deck and was intended as an aid for returning pilots to recognize the ship, CV-3.

The *Saratoga* is viewed from off the bow at the Navy Yard, Puget Sound, in a photo dated 7 September 1944, giving an idea of how the new Measure 32/11-A camouflage scheme appeared from head-on. Crewmen on the flight deck give a sense of scale.

Seen here at the Puget Sound Navy Yard on 6 September 1944, is the USS *Saratoga's* combat information center, where the locations of enemy ships, aircraft, and submarines are plotted in real time.

In this view of the forward part of the port side of *Saratoga*'s smokestack dated 6 September 1944, to the upper right the new foremast and radar equipment mounted on it have been obliterated in the photo lab. Details are visible of the frameworks at the bottoms of the SM-1 radar-antenna platform, the 36-inch searchlight platform, the Mk. 51 director tub, and the quad 40mm gun sponson. To the lower right is a shipyard crane. (San Bruno NARA, via Tracy White)

The structural foundations of the aft Mk. 37 director and the aft air-defense and director platform midway up the rear of the smokestack are viewed from the port side. Substantial bracing is present under the platform to support the weight of the platform, splinter shield, and the Mk. 37 director and its foundation. The small platform below the air-defense and director platform was the reproducer platform, with a large loudspeaker. (San Bruno NARA, via Tracy White)

The foremast, left, and front of the smokestack of USS *Saratoga* are observed from the port side in a photo dated 6 September 1944. Three heavy-duty stays, two attached to the superstructure and one to the lower front of Radar II, the small compartment on the front of the smokestack. The SK radar antenna is prominent on the platform on the foremast; behind that antenna is the YE aircraft beacon, which resembles a bow and arrow. (National Archives, San Bruno, via Tracy White)

Crewmen and civilian yard workers are preparing USS *Saratoga* for departure from the Navy Yard, Puget Sound, and a return to sea in early September 1944. The scene is on the flight deck, looking aft, with the two forward twin 5-inch/38-caliber gun mounts, the island, and the smokestack in view. Ordnance is being loaded into the magazines far below decks, and in the foreground are bombs, piles of bomb fins, and packing materials. (National Archives, San Bruno, via Tracy White)

Saratoga is viewed from off her starboard bow not long after her summer 1944 refitting at the Navy Yard, Puget Sound. The scene appears to have been at pier F-9 at Ford Island, Pearl Harbor. The newly strengthened aircraft crane is poised over an F6F. (National Museum of Naval Aviation)

Saratoga, wearing her Measure 32/11-A camouflage, lies tied up in Pearl Harbor in late 1944. Across the stern can be seen stacks of life rafts hung between the 20mm gun tubs under the flight deck overhang. (National Museum of Naval Aviation)

While conducting exercises off Hawaii on 14 October 1944, the destroyer USS *Clark* (DD-361) collided with the *Saratoga*, plowing into the carrier's port side. *Saratoga* returned to Pearl Harbor and went into dry dock, where she received temporary repairs. As seen in this photo of the ship in dry dock looking aft, two temporary patches were installed, one above the port blister and one below it on the port blister.

Deep within *Saratoga* on the second platform deck aft of the main engineering spaces is the main control room, where orders from the crew navigating the ship in the pilot house are translated into the control of the ship's power and propulsion system. In this photo, two officers in the main control room man the repeaters, which receive engine-order and steering directions from the pilot house. Despite the ship's turboelectric drive, a traditional engine-room telegraph was used. (National Archives via Rob Stern)

In a photograph dated 16 November 1944, an officer mans the control panel in the main control room of USS *Saratoga*. It was here that the electrical power generated by the power plant was regulated and routed as necessary to run the eight drive motors that powered the ship's propellers. The officers and crewmen who staffed the control room were experts at regulating the mazes of switches, buss bars, shunts, and gauges. (National Archives via Rob Stern)

The electrical power generated by the ship's four turbo-generators and alternators was transmitted to main control, from which electricity was provided to the four main drive motors located on the first platform. Part of a drive motor is shown in this photo. (National Archives via Rob Stern)

On 9 December 1944, Admiral Chester Nimitz and a subcommittee of the House Naval Affairs Committtee attended an assembly on the hangar deck of the *Saratoga*. Mounted in slings on the bulkhead in the background are spare aircraft wings of different types. (Naval History and Heritage Command)

During his 9 December 1944 visit to USS *Saratoga*, Admiral Chester Nimitz, commander in chief, Pacific Fleet (CINCPAC), accepts a piece of cake. Two days later, Nimitz attained five-star rank when President Franklin D. Roosevelt appointed him fleet admiral. (Naval History and Heritage Command)

Captain Lucian A. Moebus, left, commander of the *Saratoga*, Representative Margaret Chase Smith of Maine, and Admiral Nimitz, are on one of *Sara's* bridges. Smith had been the sponsor of legislation to create the WAVES, the women's branch of the navy. (National Archives via Rob Stern)

While supporting the invasion of Iwo Jima at 1659 on 21 February 1945, the *Saratoga* was attacked by six Japanese kamikaze aircraft. One plane was shot down before it could crash into the ship, but the other five made hits on the ship, causing extensive damage. (National Archives)

Saratoga was photographed from another ship after being hit by the kamikazes. Much smoke is coming off the forward part of the flight deck and the starboard side of the hull. The first plane penetrated the starboard side at frame 147 and exploded in the hangar. (USS *Saratoga* Association, Harold C. Cassar photo collection)

Fires rage on the forward part of *Saratoga*'s flight deck, perhaps caused by the explosion of bombs in the anchor-windlass room one level below the flight deck. Captain Moebus turned the ship from the wind to keep the flames from spreading aft on the flight deck. (USS *Saratoga* Association, Harold C. Cassar photo collection)

Fire-fighting crewmen scramble on the flight deck of *Saratoga* to combat the spread of flames during the 21 February 1945 kamikaze attack. Smoke is rising up through the deck from fires below decks. A Hellcat fighter plane is nearly fully engulfed in flames. (USS *Saratoga* Association, Harold C. Cassar photo collection)

In a view taken from the aft air-defense and director platform looking forward, with the port side of the smokestack and the port 36-inch searchlight platform to the right, firefighting crews struggle to save the *Saratoga*, spraying water and foamite fire retardant. (National Museum of Naval Aviation)

A photographer snapped this shot from the bridge of *Saratoga* at the height of the fires that threatened to engulf the ship on 21 February 1945. The last suicide plane to strike the ship crashed into the aircraft crane to the front of these twin 5-inch/38-caliber mounts. (National Archives via Rob Stern)

Emergency crewmen are making headway in fighting the fires on the forward end of the flight deck. A destroyed Grumman Hellcat lies in a heap on the flight deck near the faux elevator markings, while another Hellcat that seems to have been unscathed rests, wings folded, to the lower left. (US Naval Institute)

The destroyed Hellcat seen in the preceding photo is viewed close-up from another angle. All that is left of the aircraft crane is its base toward the lower center of the photograph. The plane that hit the crane also caused damage to the gun gallery to the lower right. (National Archives)

This quad 40mm gun mount in a gallery alongside the flight deck was savaged by the kamikaze attack. Foamite fire retardant left a white residue on the guns. The remains of one of the crewmen are visible below the rears of the receivers of the 40mm guns. (USS *Saratoga* Association, Harold C. Cassar photo collection)

Another quad 40mm gun mount is viewed in the aftermath of the 21 February 1945 kamikaze attack off Iwo Jima. The remains of a crewman are sprawled between the two pairs of guns. Clips of 40mm ammunition rounds litter the platform of the mount. (USS *Saratoga* Association, Harold C. Cassar photo collection)

Some of the dead from the 21 February attack lie in a compartment in the *Saratoga*. The toll of the attack on *Saratoga* was 62 killed, 192 wounded, and 61 missing. None of the missing were found. The kamikaze attack on *Saratoga* lasted only about three minutes. (USS *Saratoga* Association, Harold C. Cassar photo collection)

At 1630 on the day after the kamikaze attack, members of the *Saratoga*'s crew were committed to the sea in a solemn ceremony by the forward elevator on the flight deck. To the right is the firing party, who will fire a three-volley salute to the honored dead. (USS *Saratoga* Association, Harold C. Cassar photo collection)

A helmeted sailor surveys damage on the *Saratoga* after the 21 February kamikaze strike. In the foreground is an area where the steel plating of the flight deck buckled. Fires and explosions in the hangar deck and in the windlass room created tremendous damage. (USS *Saratoga* Association, Harold C. Cassar photo collection)

The forward part of the flight deck essentially was destroyed in the attack. Here, crewmen remove charred planks from a buckled section of deck. The *Saratoga*, however, was still able to recover returning aircraft on the aft part of her flight deck. (USS *Saratoga* Association, Harold C. Cassar photo collection)

Crewmen inspect the torn-up planks and deck plates on the port side of the flight deck facing aft. One of the kamikazes crashed into the forward port area of the flight deck, igniting fully fueled Hellcats ready to take off on a combat air patrol mission. (USS *Saratoga* Association, Harold C. Cassar photo collection)

A torn-up section of flight deck, shredded virtually beyond recognition, is documented in a photo taken in the aftermath of the 21 February 1945 strike. This exceeded the type of bomb damage that could be temporarily repaired so flight operations could resume. (USS *Saratoga* Association, Harold C. Cassar photo collection)

Crewmen of the *Saratoga* sort through the devastation on the main deck of the ship, underneath a large void in the flight deck. Major damage and twisted wreckage of this sort would require a visit to a naval shipyard to put the *Saratoga* back in full service. (USS *Saratoga* Association, Harold C. Cassar photo collection)

This berthing space below decks in the *Saratoga* was damaged in the kamikaze attack. A projectile appears to have crashed through the ceiling in the background, tossing around lockers, spalling paint off the steel surfaces, and tearing-up piping and overhead beams. (USS *Saratoga* Association, Harold C. Cassar photo collection)

Grumman Hellcats stored on the hangar deck of the *Saratoga* were incinerated in the 21 February 1945 kamikaze strike. Thirty-six planes assigned to the carrier were destroyed in the attack. At the time of the attack, Air Group 53 (N) was embarked on the ship. (National Museum of Naval Aviation)

After the kamikaze attack, USS *Saratoga* went into dry dock at the Navy Yard, Puget Sound, for repairs. The scene is in the anchor-windlass compartment on the main deck level facing forward; the wreckage of the flight deck has been removed in this area. (National Archives via James Noblin and Roger Torgeson)

Navy-yard workers survey the devastation in the anchor-windlass compartment in spring 1945. Although officials at the yard reported that the *Saratoga* was the most severely damaged ship they ever had repaired, repairs were completed within two months. (National Archives via James Noblin and Roger Torgeson)

USS *Saratoga* Measure 21

The Measure 32/11-A camouflage scheme on USS *Saratoga* that dated to the summer of 1944 was repainted in Measure 21, an overall Navy Blue (5-N) scheme effective against aerial observation, by February 1945. Unfortunately, the camouflage was not adequate to hide *Saratoga* from Japanese aviators, which resulted in the devastating damage depicted on the preceding pages.

Her damages from the February kamikaze attack completed, and sporting a rebuilt forward part of her flight deck, *Saratoga* undergoes full-power trials in Puget Sound on 12 May 1945. During this day's trials, one of the turbines began smoking. The bad luck continued on that day when, during test-firing of the aft twin 5-inch/38-caliber gun mount, a round exploded in one of the guns, injuring 11 crewmen.

Saratoga conducts full-power trials in Puget Sound in May 1945, a few days after the 12 May explosion in the aft twin 5-inch/38-caliber gun mount. The carrier bears the Measure 21 camouflage scheme applied in late 1944; this was the ship's final camouflage scheme.

On the same occasion as the preceding photo, *Saratoga* is viewed off the aft starboard quarter. On close inspection of the photo, the aft twin 5-inch mount is trained to starboard, and the left barrel, in which a round exploded, is no longer present.

151

USS *Saratoga* rests in port around the end of World War II. After completing her repairs at the Navy Yard, Puget Sound, in the spring of 1945, the ship did not return to combat operations. Since many other aircraft carriers of more recent vintage were now available to the U.S. Navy, the *Saratoga* was converted to a training carrier for the remainder of the war. In this color view, the ship displays her Navy Blue late-war Measure 21 camouflage scheme.

The crew of one of the *Saratoga*'s eight single-mounted 5-inch/38-caliber guns conducts exercises on 9 September 1945. The shield to the left protected some of the machinery of the gun mount. The crew, though, was fully exposed to shrapnel, splinters, and projectiles. (National Archives via Rob Stern)

A Grumman F6F-5 appears in markings for VF-58 on *Saratoga* in February 1945. The F6F-5 had a top speed of 380 miles per hour and a maximum range of 944 miles, and was armed with six .50-caliber machine guns as well as a mix of bombs and rockets.

Saratoga is docked at Ford Island, Pearl Harbor, around mid-1945. The carrier arrived in Pearl Harbor from San Francisco on 1 June 1945 ferrying a cargo of aircraft, trucks, and some 1,200 military passengers. While in Hawaiian waters, the *Saratoga* engaged in training exercises. In this photograph, twin 5-inch/38-caliber gun mount number eight, the aft twin mount, has been repaired and the left gun barrel is present; replacement of this mount, damaged in the explosion on 12 May, was effected at Pearl Harbor the week of 10 June 1945.

Saratoga was receiving a hasty, but badly needed, overhaul at Hunters Point, San Francisco, as 1943 turned to 1944. She had dropped anchor at noon on 9 December 1943, and the following morning entered drydock. While the crew took well-deserved liberty, shipyard workers updated *Saratoga*. Additional 40mm guns were added, at the cost of removing some of the 20mm mounts, added emergency diesel generators and modernized her radar. *Saratoga* left the shipyard on 2 January, and the next day stood out from the bay, bound for Pearl Harbor, arriving at that anchorage 7 January.

She sailed on 19 January with her old partner the *Princeton*, as well as *Langley*, bound for the Marshalls, striking Wortje and Taroa from 29 to 31 January, before shifting her sights on Eniwetok, which continued to be *Saratoga's* target sporadically through 28 February. It was during this time as well that Lt.JG Bill Johnson made the 75,000th successful landing on *Saratoga's* deck.

While sailing from Espiritu Santo bound for Hobart, Tasmania, *Saratoga* encountered heavy seas from 12 March to 15 March. Waves reached the flight deck, washing away not only two life rafts, but also a 40mm gun director. At Hobart, *Saratoga* received orders attaching her to the British Eastern Fleet. While on this duty she visited Colombo, Ceylon, where she received aboard the Supreme Commander of the South East Asia Area, Admiral Louis Mountbatten.

Saratoga was detached from the British fleet on 18 May 1944, and sailed to Sydney, Australia, where the crew was granted liberty as their ship was reprovisioned, before sailing on to Pearl Harbor, where she arrived on 10 June. Two days later she sailed for Bremerton, past

due for an overhaul. She entered Drydock #4 at Puget Sound Naval Shipyard on 18 June. Thoroughly overhauled and modernized, with new catapults installed and a new camouflage paint scheme applied, *Saratoga* left the drydock on 13 August, and soon began what would be her most tragic deployment.

Operating off Hawaii, on the morning of 14 October 1944, the destroyer *Clark* collided with *Saratoga,* the latter receiving minimal damage. However, the next day, an aviation fuel fire broke out, incidental to attempting temporary repairs to the collision damage. *Saratoga* entered drydock at Pearl on 1 November for permanent collision repairs, and the application of yet another camouflage scheme. At sea once again on 21 February 1945, *Saratoga* was operating off Iwo Jima and Chichi Jima, when she came under a multiple kamikaze attack. She suffered five hits in thee minutes, resulting in 123 crewmen dead or missing and extensive blast and fire damage, requiring her return to Puget Sound, where she would remain until 22 May. Officials at Puget Sound deemed *Saratoga* the most extensively damaged ship ever repaired at the yard. Given her age and wounds, she was repaired and returned to duty, not as a combat vessel, but as a training carrier.

Saratoga would end her wartime service as honorably and purposefully as she had served the nation since her 1927 commissioning. Having served as a training carrier in the waning months of WWII, she went on to take part in numerous "Magic Carpet" missions, returning many eager servicemen to the continental United States. But her age, combat damage, and advancements in naval aviation had rendered her obsolete, despite remaining one of the largest aircraft carriers afloat.

At the end of World War II, USS *Saratoga* was used to ferry Naval personnel back to the United States from the Pacific Theater. Here, with some 3,800 passengers and crewmen thronging the deck, the ship passes through the Golden Gate on 13 September 1945. (National Park Service via Jerry Leslie)

A U.S. Navy blimp flies over *Saratoga*, her flight deck packed with returning servicemen. After making the initial ferry trip with returning personnel from Hawaii to San Francisco in early September, the ship made several more such runs. (National Park Service via Jerry Leslie)

A happy-looking crowd of naval personnel about to return home from the war are gathered on the flight deck of the *Saratoga*. The ship's first ferry run in early September 1945 transported 301 Naval officers, 3,408 enlisted men, and three civilians. (National Park Service via Jerry Leslie)

USS *Saratoga* rests dockside, her flight deck thronged with returning naval personnel. The photograph was taken from the bridge looking forward. In the foreground, the palisade on the flight deck has been erected. Considerable baggage is also on deck. (National Park Service via Jerry Leslie)

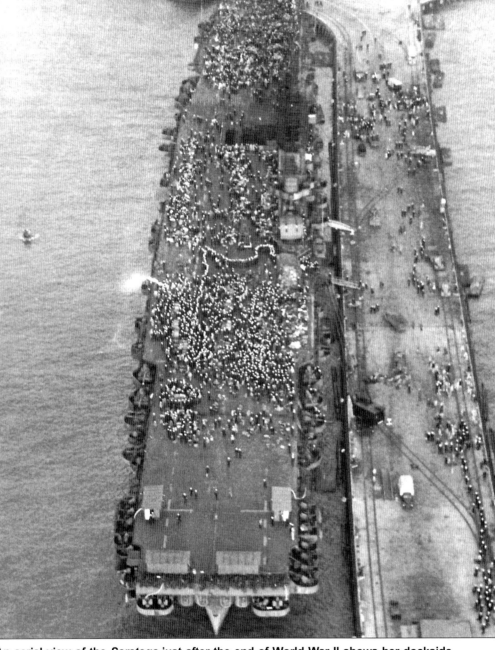

An aerial view of the *Saratoga* just after the end of World War II shows her dockside, her flight deck teeming with returning naval officers and enlisted men. At the aft end of the flight deck and on the ramp are four temporary shelters. It was rather fitting that the carrier that had won a soft spot in the hearts of her crewmen through almost two decades of service would also win a similar spot in the hearts of the men whom the carrier transported back home from the war. (National Park Service via Jerry Leslie)

155

After one final run from Hawaii in early January 1946, *Saratoga* proceeded to Hunter's Point, San Francisco and was prepared for use in the forthcoming nuclear tests at Bikini Atoll. Here, Sara is being relieved of some of her gun mounts prior to the tests. (National Park Service via Jerry Leslie)

Shipyard workers are dressing up the opening created when the aft twin 5-inch/38-caliber gun mount was removed from the flight deck. In the right background is the deckhouse on which the second from aft twin 5-inch/38-caliber mount rested. (National Park Service via Jerry Leslie)

In a photo taken at NAS Alameda on San Francisco Bay and dated 27 February 1946, twin 5-inch/38-caliber gun mount number six has been removed, but twin 5-inch mount five remains in place on the flight deck. A temporary fence is around the elevator well. (NARA via James Noblin)

Sailors and civilians wave goodbye and a Navy airship flies overhead as tugboats back USS *Saratoga* from Pier 33 at San Francisco. The carrier is preparing to proceed to Bikini Atoll for the Operation Crossroads atomic test. The date is 1 May 1946. (National Park Service via Jerry Leslie)

Saratoga steams though the Golden Gate toward her final destination, Bikini Atoll. On the port side of the flight deck amidships is a small platform that probably was installed after the war. The navy did not bother to remove most of the ship's radar antennas. (NARA San Bruno via Tracy White)

On 1 May 1946, *Saratoga* passes under the Golden Gate Bridge. The next stop would be Pearl Harbor, where the carrier arrived on 7 May. The carrier sallied out of Pearl Harbor, the site of many visits during the war, for the final time on 23 May, bound for Bikini. (National Park Service via Jerry Leslie)

In an aerial view of USS *Saratoga* departing from Pier 33 at San Francisco on 1 May 1946, it is apparent that when twin 5-inch/38-caliber gun mount number four was removed, the opening it left in the deck house it was mounted on was neatly filled with a large circular plate. Arrayed on deck are various aircraft, including Hellcats, Avengers, and Helldivers; vehicles, including Jeeps, a DUKW, tanks and artillery pieces. The effects of nuclear blasts would be tested on these objects as well as on the ship itself. (National Park Service via Jerry Leslie)

Operation Crossroads

While the three atomic bomb detonations during WWII – Trinity Site, Hiroshima, and Nagasaki – had been studied extensively, no data were available on the effect of an atomic blast on a warship, nor on the latest U.S. Army ground equipment. It was decided that three tests would be conducted in remote areas of the Pacific. Dubbed Operation Crossroads, the tests would feature an above-water blast (Able), a shallow-water detonation (Baker), and a deep-water blast (Charlie). Bikini Atoll was selected as the site for the first two, with the Charlie test, which was ultimately cancelled, to be outside the atoll. On 24 January 1946 *Saratoga* was named one of the 35 major vessels (out of a total of 200) that would serve as the target fleet. *Saratoga* was chosen because, despite her age and obsolescence, her subdivision, comprising almost 1,000 watertight compartments, as well as her underwater protection, were similar to those of the most modern U.S. warships of the era.

Saratoga was stripped of certain hardware, armament, and items deemed historically significant, such as her bell (now at the National Museum of Naval Aviation) and her silver service. Prior to her sailing from San Francisco for the final time, onto her decks were placed an assortment of Naval aircraft, as well as a range of U.S. Army vehicles and equipment, including tanks, artillery pieces, and a DUKW. Various instrumentation was placed aboard to measure the effect of the atomic blasts to which she would be subjected.

Like most of the target fleet, *Saratoga* survived the 1 July 1946 Able air blast at Bikini, though the fueled aircraft on her decks were set afire. The Baker test on 25 July 1946, however, lifted her stern 43 feet and her bow 29 feet. All aircraft and vehicles were swept from her flight deck, and her stack was washed over the side. Yet despite being only 400 yards from the blast, *Saratoga* remained afloat for eight hours before slipping beneath the surface.

Saratoga **endured two atomic blasts at Bikini Atoll. The first one, code-named Able, was an air burst on 1 July 1946. The second, called Baker, was an underwater blast on 25 July 1946, shown here.** *Saratoga* **is on the left side of the rising column of water. (US Naval Institute)**

The Baker explosion occurred at 0835. *Saratoga* **was anchored 400 yards from the epicenter; the blast shoved her a distance of 400 yards away from her anchorage. Soon, the carrier began to sink. The island and the rear part of the smokestack are still standing. (Naval History and Heritage Command)**

In this photo, only the forward part of the flight deck is still above water, the number 3 visible on it. A mass of air bubbles is churning up from the aft part of the ship. The venerable old ship sank at around 1608, almost eight hours after the atomic blast. (National Museum of Naval Aviation)

Saratoga today

During WWII, the U.S. Navy operated almost 7,000 ships, of which just over 150 were lost due to enemy action. In the years after VJ Day, most survivors of this vast armada were unceremoniously scrapped, with a handful preserved as museums and memorials.

Saratoga is somewhat among this latter group. Resting in the relatively shallow, clear waters of Bikini Atoll, *Saratoga* has welcomed numerous visitors since she slipped beneath the waves. Navy divers surveyed the wreck almost immediately after Test Baker, first descending to her wreck on 24 August 1946. These evaluation dives continued until 30 August. On 17 July 1947, as part of the Bikini Resurvey Operation, a team of U.S. government divers returned to *Saratoga* in "an effort to determine the exact cause of sinking" in the words of the Sunken Ship Inspection Plan.

Along with other vessels sunk by tests Able and Baker, *Saratoga* languished on the atoll bottom largely undisturbed until the late 1980s, when National Park Service as well as Navy Explosive Ordnance Disposal teams made additional dives. By this time the radiation hazard had largely passed, but the dangers inherent with a sunken steel vessel remained. Problems of leaking fuel oil, the weakening of the structure by rust, the lines and cables that present tanglement hazards, were compounded by the circumstances of *Saratoga's* sinking – blast damage as well as live bombs and other ordnance aboard. Despite this, *Saratoga* has become an exciting destination for advanced sport divers.

Today, the sunken ships of Bikini Atoll are available for exploration by divers. Here, a diver investigates the aft air-defense and director platform and aft Mk. 37 director, visible to the left. Toward the center is a remnant of the aft part of the smokestack. (National Park Service, Submerged Resources Center)

By the mid-1990s radioactivity at the Bikini Atoll atomic test site had abated sufficiently to allow divers to explore the sunken ships in the lagoon. Among them is the *Saratoga*, which is the largest diveable sunken ship in the world and one of only two diveable aircraft carriers. In this photo, a diver explores above the quad 40mm gun mount seen at the bottom of the photo, which is located aft of the island, visible in the background. (National Park Service, Submerged Resources Center)

The *Saratoga* was a key component in the United States' growing naval air arm from the late 1920s through World War II, serving as a training ground for many naval aviation pioneers and as a respected fighting ship. After a brief postwar interlude of bringing returning servicemen home from the war, the aging carrier was selected as part of the test fleet used to evaluate the effects on warships of the newly developed atomic bomb. Having survived the Able blast, *Saratoga* succumbed to the Baker blast on 25 July 1946. Today her hulk rests upright on the bottom of the atoll at a depth of 190 feet. Recently, *Saratoga* became a popular diving destination; her bridge is readily accessible at a depth of 40 feet. (National Park Service, Submerged Resources Center)